Religion and Democracy

Edited by

David Marquand and Ronald L Nettler

Blackwell Publishers

Copyright © The Political Quarterly Publishing Co. Ltd.

ISBN 0–631–22184–0

First published 2000

Blackwell Publishers
108 Cowley Road, Oxford, OX4 1JF, UK.

and
350 Main Street,
Malden, MA 02148, USA.

British Library Cataloguing in Publication Data
A catalogue record for this book is available from the British Library

Library of Congress Cataloging in Publication Data
Cataloging-in-Publication data applied for

Printed in the UK by Cambrian Printers, Aberystwyth

CONTENTS

Notes on Contributors

Colin Crouch is Professor of Comparative Social Institutions at the European University Institute, Florence, and external scientific member of the Max Planck Institute for Society Research, Cologne. He is Chairman of the editorial board of *The Political Quarterly*. His recent works include *Industrial Relations and European State Traditions* (1993); *Are Skills the Answer?* (with David Finegold and Mari Sako) (1999); and *Social Change in Western Europe* (1999).

Paul Hirst is Professor of Social Theory at Birkbeck College University of London and Academic Director of the London Consortium Graduate Programme in Humanities and Cultural Studies. He is author of, among other works, The Pluralist Theory of the State; Selected Writings of G. D. H. Cole, J. N. Figgis and H. J. Laski (1989), Associative Democracy (1994) and From Statism to Pluralism (1997).

John Keane is Professor of Politics at the Centre for the Study of Democracy. He is author of many books, including the prize-winning *Tom Paine: A Political Life* (1995), and his most recent work, *Vaclav Havel: A Political Tragedy in Six Acts* (1999). Among his many current research interests are the history of secularism and the philosophy and politics of Islam.

Ronald L. Nettler is Fellow and Tutor in Oriental Studies, Mansfield College, Oxford, and Hebrew Centre Lecturer in Oriental Studies, Oxford University. His main interest is in Islamic and Jewish religious thought, medieval and modern.

Dr Emanuele Ottolenghi is Junior Research Fellow in Israel Studies at the Middle East Centre of St Antony's College, and at the Oxford Centre for Hebrew and Jewish Studies.

Harold Perkin is Emeritus Professor Of Social History at Northwestern University. His most recent book is *The Third Revolution: Professional Elites in the Modern World* (Routledge, 1996).

Susanne Hoeber Rudolph and Lloyd Rudolph are both Professors at the University of Chicago. Their field is modern India.

Timothy Samuel Shah is a Ph.D. candidate in Government at Harvard University. He is Research Advisor to a research project on Evangelical Christianity and Political Democracy in Asia, Africa and Latin America, organised by the International Fellowship of Evangelic Mission Theologians and funded by The Pew Charitable Trusts; and also a Reseach Fellow at The Ethics and Public Policy Center, Washington, D.C.

Sami Zubaida teaches Politics and Sociology at Birkbeck College. His research and writing are on religion, ethnicity and nationalism in Middle East politics, and on food and culture. Author of *Islam, the People and the State* (1993) and co-editor with R. Tapper of *Culinary Cultures of the Middle East* (1994).

© The Political Quarterly Publishing Co. Ltd. 2000
Published by Blackwell Publishers, 108 Cowley Road, Oxford OX4 1JF, UK and 350 Main Street, Malden, MA 02148, USA

Foreword

IN *Democracy in America*, perhaps the most penetrating analysis of the social and cultural foundations of pluralist democracy ever written, Alexis de Tocqueville suggested that—contrary to European presuppositions— American experience showed that religion and democracy could perfectly well go together. Indeed, the Americans themselves believed that the health of their republican institutions owed much to their religious beliefs. But there was a crucial, if paradoxical, proviso. Church and state had to be kept apart. Though de Tocqueville did not say this in so many words, the picture he painted was one of a tacit bargain through which religion kept out of politics, and politics did not interfere with religion. It was because the American clergy had understood this that their role in American society was so notable. Their influence over their flocks was a function of their political circumspection.

I learned with surprise that they filled no public appointments; I did not see one of them in the administration, and they are not even represented in the legislative assemblies. In several states the law excludes them from political life; public opinion excludes them in all. And when I came to enquire into the prevailing spirit of the clergy, I found that most of its members seemed to retire from their own accord from the exercise of power, and that they made it the pride of their profession to abstain from politics . . .

. . . They saw that they must renounce their religious influence if they were to strive for political power, and they chose to give up the support of the state rather than to share its vicissitudes.[1]

100 years ago, most secular progressives took it for granted that the pattern which de Tocqueville thought he saw in the United States would gradually become universal. For them, modernity implied, among other things, the political marginalisation of religion. Religious beliefs might survive. They might even prosper, as de Toqueville believed they prospered in the United States; but they would slowly fade out of the public sphere. Faith would be a private matter, with no political significance. Politics would be about issues— the promotion of prosperity, the distribution of resources, the clash of classes, the rise and fall of nations—to which religious affiliation would be irrelevant.

Manifestly, this has not happened. Even in the United States, for many the paradigmatic modern society, the political role of religion remains both obtrusive and critical. Indeed, it is in many ways more obtrusive today than de Tocqueville believed it to be 170 years ago. Certainly, the clergy— or at any rate a significant part of it—no longer exhibits the political circumspection that struck him so forcibly. As the unfortunate Senator

© The Political Quarterly Publishing Co. Ltd. 2000
Published by Blackwell Publishers, 108 Cowley Road, Oxford OX4 1JF, UK and 350 Main Street, Malden, MA 02148, USA

McCain discovered on super-Tuesday 2000, the religious right now has an arm-lock on the Republican Party; and as President Clinton proved during the Monica Lewinsky affair, the public display of an unctuous religiosity, which would invite contempt or derision in most of western Europe, may be the best way for a politician caught with his pants down to shore up his political fortunes. Thomas Jefferson's gentlemanly Enlightenment scepticism would probably be a disqualification for the White House today.

In different ways, and to different degrees, India, Israel and the Islamic world display a similar pattern. Western Europe appears to be an exception. Despite the continued existence of important Christian Democratic parties in some west European countries, and despite the continued influence of Catholic social teaching on the economic and political cultures of the countries concerned, organised religion almost certainly plays a smaller role in politics in 2000 over most of the territory of the European Union than it did in 1950. Yet even in Western Europe, a growing Islamic minority calls the existing, fuzzy and historically contingent boundaries between the domain of faith and the domain of politics into question. In the world as a whole—in the globalising world of the twenty-first century, with its accelerating international competition, its massive transnational capital flows and its formidable multi-national media empires—the old secularist expectation that progressive modernisation would slowly banish religion from the public sphere has been spectacularly belied by events. The world of the internet is also the world of militant Islam, of the Israeli fundamentalist right and of the Indian BJP. In Benjamin Barber's provocative terminology, 'jihad' and 'McWorld' have gone together.[2]

This book is intended to contribute to the growing volume of public debate which this remarkable—and perhaps alarming—coincidence has provoked. It stems from a conference organised jointly by THE POLITICAL QUARTERLY and the Religion and Democracy programme at Mansfield College, Oxford, in September, 1999. The object of the conference was to explore the contested and fluctuating relationship between religious belief and pluralist democracy, in the context of an increasingly global economy and culture. More particularly it was to ask whether the continued, and in many cases enhanced, political intrusiveness of religion endangers the foundations of democratic governance.

To that question, most of the contributors to this book have given (implicitly if not explicitly) a relatively optimistic answer. It can be summarised as follows. Even in the absence of a Tocquevillian bargain keeping church and state apart, religion and democracy can co-exist. Communities of faith do not necessarily imperil the foundations of pluralist democracy by seeking to pursue essentially religious agendas through political action. Nor does globalisation inevitably provoke a democracy-threatening explosion of religious militancy. But here too there is a proviso. As Paul Hirst argues in his chapter on the pluralism of J. N. Figgis and its implications for modern, culturally heterogeneous societies, a degree of mutual tolerance, or at least of mutual self-restraint, is indispensable. Religious groups have to accept the right of other religious groups—and by the same token, the right of the non-religious—to abide by their own values. (The second may well be harder to achieve in practice than the first.) The 'cultural federalism' which Susanne and Lloyd Rudolph describe in their chapter on India is, of course, the product of specific Indian conditions, and it would be wrong to see it as a model for the rest of the world, but in some respects, at least, it seems to be an example of what Figgis had in mind. And federalism depends, among other things, on the willingness of the federated to respect the boundaries between each other.

Such self-restraint may, however, be difficult to achieve evenly and with some assurance of the stability and continuity that the long-term co-existence of religion and democracy requires. For its achievement depends on the willingness of religious communities to accept a new (modern) curbing of some of religion's 'natural inclinations' (or at least of inclinations which for most of its history have been central to religious life). Pre-modern religion was necessarily political and public, in the sense that it sought a natural existence in the sphere of public institutions which organised human existence. Pre-modern religion also, in many cases, tended towards exclusivism, assuming the possibility of only one true tradition.

These were the hallmarks of religion in Western countries, in the Islamic world and in many other places until the early twentieth century. The process whereby these features met their match in twentieth-century modernity began, of course, several centuries earlier in Europe. From the early seventeenth century the questioning of received truths and doctrines in science, philosophy and religion, combined with related structural changes in material life and politics, challenged the pre-modern political and public face of religion and the exclusivist religious axiom. The battle lines were thus drawn and in the West the struggle was thus conducted. It still continues, with varying intensity in different places. Why the intensity is greater in some places than in others is a question for discussion, as Harold Perkin shows in his chapter on 'fundamentalist' religion in the United States. Here the frankly political face of religion seems more prominent than in most other Western countries, despite seemingly thoroughgoing secularisation. But whatever the intensity and stage of the process in a particular country, for the West it is an indigenous process, organic to Europe, to the United States and to their tributary nations. If tension remains between certain religious tendencies and pluralist democracy, it is a familiar tension rooted in now institutionalised habits and outlooks. In the non-West, however, in particular in the Islamic world, the issue was forced on religion in an even more brutal way: Western hegemony (political, economic and ideological) as an alien force imposed its influence, engendering a tension parallel to that in the West, but more highly accelerated and lacking indigenous roots. In both cases, certain reactions have been prominent. 'Fundamentalism' in the West as well as the non-West may be seen here as a particularly strident attempt of religion to reassert its old political privilege. 'Personalisation' of religion, on the other hand, drawn from the existing elements in a particular tradition (e.g. mysticism or pietistic personal morality), depoliticises it and thus renders it what we call 'liberal' and perhaps more amenable to pluralism. This is a response which is, of course, opposite to 'fundamentalism'. Such a trend is increasingly prominent in the Islamic world, as Ronald Nettler shows in his chapter on the Tunisian Muslim modernist Mohamed Talbi. Talbi, like his counterparts in other Muslim countries, totally detaches religion from politics and envisions a pluralist world of religions where all faiths are equal paths to God. This intellectual trend grows more prominent, while at the same time 'fundamentalism' in the Islamic world is, on another level, widespread, as Sami Zubaida shows in his chapter on Islamic politics in certain Middle Eastern countries.

The rich variety of this book cannot be captured within the boundaries of a short introduction. We have sought, rather, to provide a general context both for the contents of the book and, not least, for the wider debate to which the book is intended to contribute. We recognise that some important themes have not been addressed here. We do believe, however, that we have offered some important perspectives through which an understanding of all the chapters may be enhanced.

D.M.
R.N.

Notes

1 Alexis de Tocqueville, *Democracy in America*, ed. Alan Ryan, Everyman's Library, 1994, pp. 309–312.
2 Benjamin Barber, *Jihad vs. McWorld*, New York, Times Books, 1995.

SECULARISM?

JOHN KEANE

In his stimulating lectures on the Christianisation of the Roman world, Professor Peter Brown shows that during the fourth and fifth centuries various Christian sources nurtured the tale of the absolute triumph of Christianity over paganism.[1] According to this tale, which in retrospect resembles a simple-minded dogma, the end of paganism occurred with the coming of Christ to earth. After He was raised on Calvary, heaven and earth rang with the crash of falling temples. The subsequent alliance of the Christian Church with Christian emperors—an alliance defined and defended, for instance, by St Augustine's attack on smoking altars and other pagan rites—represented a final push to victory, a mop-up operation that brought Christian triumph and permanent defeat for the shadowy empire of the demons.

The Christianisation narrative, the tale of the conquering of the temporal world by the spiritual, has reappeared under modern conditions, in mirror-image form, in the doctrine of the secularisation of the world. Especially among intellectual defenders of secularism who think of themselves as democrats, there is a strong tendency to dogmatise secularism by supposing its long-term victory over the process of Christianisation. Secularists come in many different shapes and sizes, it is true.[2] Yet for many 'no secularism; no democracy' is something of a sacred equation. Analytic distinctions, for instance between secularism as an ideal-type and as a set of moral recommendations, are typically blurred in favour of a large narrative: secularists suppose that during modern times, and especially during the past several generations, religious illusions have gradually disappeared. Men and women have left God not for other gods, but for no god. This trend is said to have many causes, including the actualisation in higher form of the Christian spirit (as Hegel originally argued). But it is said to have had one principal effect: 'the modern West has produced an increasing number of individuals who look upon the world and their own lives without the benefit of religious interpretations.'[3] The outcome is said to be self-reinforcing—secularisation produces a crisis of credibility of religion, which in turn feeds 'a widespread collapse of the plausibility of traditional religious definitions of reality'.[4] A virtuous circle results, many secular observers conclude. The extrusion of religious sentiments from such domains as law, government, party politics, and education—commonly called the separation of church and state—not only releases citizens from metaphysical prejudice. The normative ideal of secularism, the growing confidence in the separation of church and state and the confinement of religious belief to the private sphere, is a positive substitute for God. The decline of religiosity actually strengthens citizens'

© The Political Quarterly Publishing Co. Ltd. 2000
Published by Blackwell Publishers, 108 Cowley Road, Oxford OX4 1JF, UK and 350 Main Street, Malden, MA 02148, USA

capacities to live in less biased, more rational ways; they become freer to run their own lives face-to-face with earthly experiences. God's departure from the world even promotes open-minded tolerance, itself a vital ingredient of a pluralist democracy. The modern quest for personal meaning and salvation is transformed into the 'invisible religion' of 'self-expression'.

Despite mounting challenges to its hegemony, the conventional doctrine of secularism remains confident, no doubt in part because its intellectual roots run deep. Surprisingly, a comprehensive scholarly genealogy of these roots remains unwritten, a gap that is symbolised by Hermann Luebbe's flawed account of the concept of secularisation.[5] Yet it is clear that the normative belief that the modern world is irreversibly destroying its religious foundations in favour of secularity, and that destination is constructive, is a child of mid-nineteenth-century Europe, while the concept of 'the secular', which is unique to European civilisation, is far older.

Ever since the adoption under Constantine of Christianity as the official religion of the Empire, the relationship between spiritual and temporal—secular—power has been controversial. As far back as the late thirteenth-century, the adjective 'secular' (from the Latin *saecularis*) was first used in English, often with negative connotations, to distinguish clergy living and working in the wider medieval world from 'religious' clergy who lived in monastic seclusion. William of Ockham and John Wycliffe, writing in the next century, strengthened this sense of the word secular by distinguishing institutions concerned with civil, lay and temporal matters from others which were clearly religious or 'spiritual'. It was in this same sense that the earliest references were made to 'the secular arm' (from the Latin *brachium seculare*) of civil power invoked by the Church to punish offenders, and to the figure of the 'secular abbot', a person who was the beneficiary of the title of abbot and enjoyed part of the revenues, but who was himself neither a monk nor entitled to exercise the functions of an abbot.

During the sixteenth century, these originally neutral or negative connotations of 'the secular' as the temporal domain of 'the worldly' not subject directly to religious rule—the domain of the non-ecclesiastical, non-religious, or non-sacred—weakened. The term 'secular' began to lose its association with profanity or outright Godlessness. It also underwent modernisation. The word 'secular' was flung into motion and used to describe a world thought to be in motion. To 'secularise' (from the French *seculariser*) meant to make someone or something secular. It meant converting them from ecclesiastical to civil use or possession, while 'secularisation' connoted a process of reducing the influence of religion, as when the term was used in legal and ecclesiastical circles to describe the transfer of religious institutions or property to lay ownership or temporal use. This is the sense in which Dr Johnson's *Dictionary* (first published in 1755) defined secularity as 'Worldliness; attention to the things of the present life', 'secularise' as 'to convert from spiritual appropriations to common use' and 'to make worldly', and 'secularisation' as the 'Act of secularising'.

Although these neologists did not know it, they were preparing the intellectual ground for the seeds of the secularist belief that took root in mid-nineteenth-century Europe and has flourished until our times: the belief that the Church and the world are caught up in an historic struggle in which slowly, irreversibly worldliness is getting the upper hand. Early examples of this intellectual trend included Feuerbach's insistence that religion itself teaches atheism, since religion in its essence supposes nothing else than the truth and divinity of 'human nature'[6]; William Lecky's confident summary of the triumph in Europe of the 'spirit of Rationalism', the weakening 'spirit of persecution', and the advancing 'secularisation of politics'[7]; and the strikingly original, bible-smashing doctrine of secularism that was pushed to the front of the political stage by George J. Holyoake, Charles Bradlaugh and others, according to whom the decline of religion should be reinforced by efforts to ensure that morality is concerned with the well-being of human beings in the present life, to the exclusion of all considerations drawn from belief in God and the afterlife.

Nietzsche and the Death of God

Much the same theme is evident in Friedrich Nietzsche's *Fröhliche Wissenschaft* (section 125), which contains a chilling account of a madman, lantern in hand in broad daylight, rushing to the town marketplace, shouting in a loud voice: 'I am looking for God! I am looking for God!' Bystanders burst into laughter at the innocent absurdity of the madman, who nevertheless persisted. He reacted with a pained expression, followed by a string of piercing questions. 'Where has God gone?', he cried out. 'I will tell you. We have killed him—you and I! We are all his murderers. But how did we do it? How could we drink up the sea? Who gave us the sponge to wipe out the whole horizon? What did we do, when we unchained this earth from its sun? Where is it moving to now? Away from all suns? Backwards, sideways, forwards, in every direction? Is there an above and below any more? Are we not wandering as through infinite nothingness? Does empty space not breathe upon us now? Has it not become colder? Is not night coming and ever more night? Must we not light lanterns at noon? Do we not hear the noise of the grave-diggers, as they bury God? Do we not smell God decaying?—Gods too decay! God is dead. God stays dead. And we have killed him.' The crowd in the market-place fell silent. The madman persisted. 'How shall we console ourselves, chief of all murderers? The holiest and most powerful that the world has ever possessed has ebbed its blood away beneath our knives—who will wipe this blood from our fingers? What water can make us clean? What atonements and sacred rites will we have to invent? Is not the greatness of this deed too great for us? Must we not ourselves become gods, in order to seem worthy of it? There never was a greater deed, and because of it all who are born after us are part of a higher history than ever was before!' The madman then lapsed into silence, watched by the shocked listeners, who pressed backwards as he flung his lantern to the ground, shattering its glass, muttering: 'I come too early, it is not yet my time. This monstrous event is still on the way—it has not yet penetrated men's ears. Lightning and thunder need time, the light of the stars needs time, deeds need time, even after they have been done, in order to be seen and heard. This deed is still further from men than the remotest stars—and yet they have done it.' The story goes that later that day the madman wandered into several of the town's churches singing his requiem *aeternam deo*. When led out and questioned he replied by asking just one question: 'What are the churches, if not the tombs and sepulchres of God?'

Nietzsche's story of the madman's announcement of the death of God has often been interpreted as prophetic—as a pronouncement that summarised and spells out the destiny of two thousand years of western history (as Heidegger proposed) and that serves as an accurate prognosis of the coming of a fully secular world so stripped of religious illusions and foundational certainties that human beings are condemned to run their own lives face to face with the experience of nothingness. Yet it is easy to see that the early protagonists of the view that the modern world is irreversibly destroying its religious foundations with the acid of secularity typically pursued their case with equal measures of presumption, prediction and prescription, and that such presumption in turn has fed academic conclusions of the kind drawn by Samuel P. Huntington. 'Western Christianity is historically the single most important characteristic of Western civilization', he writes, adding that Western Christianity displays the *unique* dualism between God and Caesar, church and state, spiritual and temporal authority, a dualism that is essential for democracy to flourish.[8]

Aided by such conclusions and abetted by large quantities of academic research, secularists have powerfully pointed to the empirical findings in their favour. They ignore the elementary point that nearly all actually existing democracies live without the church-state dualism. Secularists instead insist on looking at other evidence, for instance that drawn from the oldest parliamentary democracy in the world, Britain. Almost half of the adult population in Britain and fully three-quarters of its younger people never go to church at all, we are told. And consider the other facts: two-thirds of citizens in Britain think that religion is generally in decline; a mere quarter of them consider this 'bad in any way'; while the proportion (currently one-third) affirming that Jesus was 'just a man' is on the rise, as is the sizeable majority (currently three-quarters) who deny the existence of the devil.[9]

Contemporary political theorists who favour secularity typically cite such evidence to refine their case for secularity by pointing to the political advantages of the secularisation of modern life. Charles Taylor, for example, has recently argued for the complementarity of a secular civil society and political democracy by highlighting the etymology of the word *saeculum*, which although of uncertain origin is regularly used in classical Latin texts to mean 'of or belonging to an age or long period', as in descriptions of so-called 'secular games' (from the Latin *ludi saeculares*) that lasted three days and three nights and were celebrated once in every 'age' or period of 120 years. In Christian usage, Taylor points out, *saeculum* connoted 'the temporal' and, hence, the world as opposed to the church. He tries to develop this theme, insisting that the modern experience of secular time stands opposed to the logic of divine time—God's time, time as eternity, the gathering of time into a unity based on a founding act that dictates the meaning of subsequent events. The positing of time as profane, such that events otherwise unrelated by cause or substantive meaning are linked by virtue of their occurrence at the same point in a single time line, militates against the idea of society as constituted by metasocial principles, such as the Will of God. Secular time instead nurtures the capacity for synoptic modes of representation or 'world pictures' (*Weltbilder*, as Heidegger called them in *Holzwege* [1950]). These synopses in turn nurture the political principle, vital for public life in a democracy, that the interaction of speaking and acting citizens within a worldly public sphere anchored in a civil society is primary, overriding all other competing foundational principles.[10]

The Jeffersonian Compromise

A different, but parallel case for secularity has been put recently by Richard Rorty, who defends a version of what he calls the Jeffersonian compromise.[11] Modern democracies, Rorty argues, should 'privatise religion without trivialising it'. The religious experience is appropriate for 'what we do with our aloneness' and citizens living together within an open civil society are certainly entitled to freedom of religious worship. But the problem is that religion usually functions, especially outside the religious community to which believing citizens belong, as a 'conversation stopper'. Communication among citizens is threatened by the silence, antagonism, bigotry and threats of violence nurtured by the dogmatic reference to religious fundamentals. A democratic polity thus has no choice but to enforce a pact: religious believers must be guaranteed their freedom to worship their God in private in exchange for non-believers' entitlement to live without religious bigotry and deception within the public domains of civil society and the state.

Rorty's defence of secularism is vulnerable to the *tu quo que* objection that in certain contexts the proposed Jeffersonian compromise is itself a conversation stopper; Taylor's bold, if rarefied description of the logic of the modern public sphere is similarly exposed to the historian's objection that, in every known case, religious discourse was a basic precondition of the rise of early modern public spheres, which correspondingly displayed strong traces of Christianity in such matters as constitutional protection of free speech, blasphemy laws, religious holidays and public prayers. Such queries can be set aside to consider instead the more consequential objection that contemporary defenders of the doctrine of secularism exaggerate the durability and openmindedness of 'secular' ideals and institutions; and that they fail to provide a more democratic understanding of religion and politics; because they cannot see that the principle of secularism is itself self-contradictory and, hence, unable in practice to provide relatively stable guidelines for citizens interacting freely within the laws and institutions of democratic civil societies and polities.

It is true that contemporary secularism is not about to collapse under the weight of its own contradictions, in no small measure because it has nurtured a shared sense among citizens and representatives, in the old democracies at least, that the bigotry and bloodshed of the old Judaeo-Christian struggles for power necessarily belong to the past. The perception that secularity is a key organising principle of an open, non-violent civil society is indeed anchored in deep time, and in surprising ways that are still poorly understood. A convincing genealogy of the birth and maturation of the modern ideal of civil society would need carefully to examine the various 'pathways' that led towards the politically established division between 'the secular' and 'the spiritual'. One such pathway was pioneered in Marsilius of Padua's *Defender of the Peace* (1324) and developed in William of Ockham's *A Short Discourse on the Tyrannical Government* (1334–1347?), which vigorously attacks absolute papal power by distinguishing secular and religious institutions and pleading for their non-violent mediation. Another pathway, one that comprises what might be called the dialectics of civil society and secularity, explicitly began with the first appearance together in Latin of the terms civil society and fanatic as *societas civilis* and *homo fanaticus* in early sixteenth-century commentaries on Aristotle's *Politics* written by Luther's friend and supporter, the German Protestant Reformer, Philipp Melanchthon. In various texts, including his principal work, *Loci communes theologici* (first published in 1518), Melanchthon criticised the fanaticism of the Anabaptists, who had wreaked havoc in the German lands in their efforts to establish the kingdom of Münster. 'Political order,' he wrote in 1545, 'is good, beautiful, pleasant to humankind, a singular work of God, who wishes men to live under common laws in civil societies'. Here the classical meaning of *societas civilis*—a type of political association which places its members under the influence of its laws and thereby ensures peaceful order and good government—is contrasted with the behaviour of raving fanatics, whose 'selves' are swallowed up in the beloved Truth that others, who perforce are doomed to annihilation, seek to ignore, reject, or combat. Fanatics have neither need to discover what is true nor to tread the mystic's solitary path through the darkness of night towards God. Fanatics are certain that they enjoy an immediate and unmediated kind of total certainty about the world, and it is this certitude that possesses them, and violently flings them into and against the world, with the aim of establishing a new world, without delay. Against such violent impatience, Melanchthon recommended the non-violent, political and legal order of civil society. So too did his friend Luther, who recommended a civil sword through the heart of all fanatical extremists. Although the kingdom of Christ was not of this world, Luther reasoned, Christ's name could not be invoked in calls to destroy earthly kingdoms by the sword. Note the brand new meaning of civil society: In the Reformation struggle against the Roman Catholic Church, fanatics are those who fail to recognise that the City of God requires the necessary mediating role on earth of civil society. The City of God requires Civil Society.

Formulations of this kind were to prove seminal in the history of modern civil societies. By synthesising Augustine and Aristotle, *The City of God* with *The Politics*, sixteenth-century Protestant thinkers not only helped in the rescue of the category of *societas civilis* that had begun during the first quarter of the fifteenth century by figures such as the Florentine civic humanist, Leonardi Bruni. The legitimation of *societas civilis* as the antidote of religious fanaticism paved the way, intellectually speaking, for the various arguments for toleration of (some) religious differences within the Earthly City of civil society. The earthly privileging of civil society also served unintentionally to fuel a dispute between the two swords, temporal and spiritual. Was the Church entitled to wield the temporal sword? Were the political authorities of civil society instead entitled to free themselves from the spiritual sword?

In practice, the controversy between the two swords produced a very wide spectrum of political positions, ranging from Caesaro-Papism to secularism, with the latter (according to secularists) slowly getting the upper hand through the course of the modernisation process. The dialectics of religion and civil society may well be turning out differently than they suppose. The victory of the forces favouring the 'privatisation' of religion within civil society may yet prove to be temporary and (considered as an episode in the complex history of modern religious politics) fleeting. This is because secularist ideals and institutions tend to produce a string of difficulties— three are examined below—that check their visibility and even provoke demands for terminating secularism.

Competition, civility and indifference

The most obvious example is the self-contradictory effects of freedom of religious association. It is commonly said by secularists that democracy requires the separation of church and state and the confinement of organised religion and religious discourse to the civil domain. Secularisation requires that citizens be emancipated from state and ecclesiastical *diktat*; they should be free to believe or to worship according to their conscience and ethical judgments. Render until Caesar the things that are Caesar's means: Caesar has no direct business in things that are not Caesar's. In practice, such religious freedom presupposes an open and tolerant civil society within whose plural structures and spaces citizens are required to avoid bitterness and bloodletting so that each can enjoy freedom from others' dogmatic beliefs and codes of conduct. In other words, secularity requires citizens to agree to disagree about religion, which ultimately means, as Voltaire spelled out in *Traité sur la Tolerance* (1763), that there must be at least some civil spaces in which religion plays little or no role at all. Religious freedom requires more than toleration, that is, disapproval or disagreement coupled with an unwillingness to take action against those who are looked down upon, with disfavour, in the interest of some ethico-political principle. Religious freedom requires religious indifference. Citizens must tolerate each others' different religious dispositions by accepting that every sect is a moral and political check upon its neighbour, and that peaceful competition, civility and indifference towards the passions of others is as wholesome in religion as in the world of commerce and exchange.

The implied agnosticism and potential atheism of secularism is a godsend to religious believers. Convinced that secularisation potentially marginalises or destroys religiosity, they take advantage of the freedom of association provided by civil society to protest against the perceived decline of religion.[12] Here it is worth noting that George Bernard Shaw's famous remark that when God is dead atheism dies as well, is not quite right, sociologically speaking. When God dies, it can be said, atheism dies and so God is reborn. why?

The contemporary rebirth of God through protest assumes two basic forms. Some, working for a this-worldly religion, emphasise that religion has to do with the whole of life. They warn that Christians should not become like the rich man who pretended not to know the beggar Lazarus lying at his gate. The life of Christ should instead be imitated: ethical concern must be extended to the hungry, the needy, the homeless, those without proper medical care, above all, to those without hope of a better future. In some versions, God even becomes multicultural, black-skinned and of female gender. There are others who protest against the perceived triumph of secularism by working for a more other-worldly religion. Moved by Christ's comment to Pilate that His kingdom is not of this world, they emphasise the importance of spiritual outreach, faith and zeal. These new religious believers lay stress on such principles as the Bible as revelation, the atoning sacrifice of Jesus on the cross, and the imminent second coming of Christ. Each of these tenets is linked in turn to the importance of preserving the family, morality, and country. Private belief is not enough; believers are called to witness before others in public, through such forums as 'house churches' and public spectacles, in which the born-again discard their worldly cares—sometimes taking off their dark glasses and rising from their wheelchairs—to proclaim the glory of God.

Such public reaffirmations of religious ethics, 'puffs of the Zeitgeist' as Hannah Arendt once called them,[13] are nowadays commonplace in open societies, not least because secularising civil societies display a second contradiction: their propensity to replace religiosity with existential uncertainty prompts the return of the sacred in everyday life. Modern civil societies, ideal-typically conceived, comprise multiple webs of 'fluid' social institutions whose dynamism and complexity prevent citizens from fully comprehending, let alone grasping the social totality within which they are born, grow to maturity and die.[14] Citizens' consequent sense of uncertainty about such matters as investment and employment, the quality of schooling and the shifting patterns of personal identity and household obligations makes them prone to stress and confusion and, hence, prone to involvement in shock-absorbing institutions, of which churches, sects and crusades remain leading examples, especially in times of personal crisis.

In a stressed and strained world, as Montesquieu pointed out in *l'Esprit des Lois*, religious movements and institutions can appeal to individuals' base instincts, like the false pride that stems from supposedly being among the select few, or personal envy of the magnificent wealth and power of highly visible churches. But religious institutions and movements regularly have more positive effects, especially when they serve as living reminders of the importance of solidarity among the shaken. They do so in several positive ways. Religiosity helps to keep open individuals' emotional channels to reservoirs of morality consisting of invented traditions such as 'family life' and the belief that if God is dead, then nothing remains but an indifferent void, the meaningless universe of cell-reproduction and oscillating electrons and protons. In a world dominated by secular time, furthermore, religiosity offsets boredom. It also heightens the sense of mysterious importance of life's rites of passage by baptising such events as birth, marriage and death in the waters of theological time, thereby reminding mortal human beings, existentially speaking, that life is an inevitable defeat. And since the members of civil societies typically experience at least something of what Heinrich von Kleist called the 'fragile constitution of the world', they are prone to experience (and take comfort in) the feeling of awe and absolute dependence upon another, larger order of existence that is thought to be anterior to human reflection, speech and interaction: a world that encourages mere mortals to feel that they bob up and down for a while on a sea that is tens of thousands of fathoms deep.

The return of the sacred admittedly assumes motley forms. Each, however, displays the shared experience of wonder and reverence for the world ('the assurance of things hoped for, the conviction of things not seen' [Hebrews 11.1]) that Friedrich Schleiermacher (in *Über die Religion* [1799]) considered to be the quintessence of religion. The return of the sacred is nowadays evident in such religious initiatives as the Sea of Faith network and Reconstructionist Judaism; in the fascination with the Dalai Lama, the I Ching and the Bhagwan and other Eastern religions and occult practices; and in the surprising opinion poll findings in the most secular countries that clear majorities (around 75 per cent in Britain) believe in 'religion' and the afterlife. The sacred has also returned during the past half-century as an inference drawn in certain quarters of scientific research (as Einstein put it) that 'a Spirit is manifest in the laws of the Universe, a spirit vastly superior to that of man and one in the face of which, with our modest powers, we should feel humble.' And the embrace of the sacred is evident in various philosophical and political warnings that secularism succours anthropocentrism, which seduces Humanity into thinking that it can play God and so do anything it likes with the worlds of inner and outer nature. Jacques Maritain's *The Twilight of Civilisation* is an early example of this line of thinking.

A more recent instance is Václav Havel's efforts to redefine democracy as a political system which cultivates a shared sense of the fallibility of human beings living in the natural world. Democracy, he argues, is 'humility towards the order and beauty of nature, as well as humility towards the beauty of things created by previous generations.'[15]

Perhaps the most strikingly contradictory, self-paralysing feature of secularism is its theoretical and practical affinity with political despotism. Secularists will likely consider this remark odd, perhaps even blasphemous. They would insist that there have been liberating, free-thinking forms of secularism. Drawing on the case of mid-Victorian Britain, for example, they would point out that secularism has been a synonym for democratic expressions of popular radicalism that resembled a cross between a workingmen's club and a sectarian chapel, wherein the word secularity meant openness to reason, willingness to compromise, freedom from bigotry and, thus, the institutional separation of church and state. The observation is undoubtedly warranted. With some justification as well, scholars such as John Neville Figgis have traced the roots of the doctrine of secularism to the justified fears of late medieval religioners—William of Ockham's *Octo quaestiones de potestate papae* (1334–1347?) is a pathbreaking example—that matters of religion and conscience were slipping into the hands of political classes who themselves refused to allow that their power merely existed on sufferance of the spiritual powers. Yet one trouble with the view that secularisation equals the struggle for freedom of expression and toleration of differences is its failure to spot the inherent dogmatism of secularism. It is not only that various political attempts (in France, Turkey and elsewhere) to institutionalise secularism have been so riddled with violence and coercion that they qualify as experiments in 'internal colonialism' (Catherine Audard).[16] Nor is it only, at the level of principle, that the early (Christian) advocates of secular freedoms typically denied others—Jews (children of the Devil) and Roman Catholics (members of the body of a prostitute), for instance—such freedoms, as if otherwise benign secularists had suffered a temporary failure of imagination, courage or will in extending their own universal principles to others. The problem actually runs deeper. For the principle of secularism, which 'represents a realisation of crucial motifs of Christianity itself' (Bonhöffer), is arguably founded upon a sublimated version of the Christian belief that Christianity is 'the religion of religions' (Schleiermacher), and that Christianity is entitled to decide for non-Christian others what they can think or say—or even whether they are capable of thinking and saying anything at all.

Muslims and Secularists

The inbuilt hostility towards Muslims of the normative ideal of secularism is the most worrying contemporary example of such dogmatism. There are two obvious clues to this extant hostility. One is that many otherwise 'unreligious' and tolerant citizens of countries such as the United State, France, and Germany treat the growing numbers of Muslims—over 20 millions in the European Union alone—who now permanently reside within the old democracies with quiet aversion, deep suspicion, or even thuggish belligerence, it is as if tolerant secularists must always stumble into *faux pas*, prevaricate or become bigots when confronted with veil-wearing, halal meat, talk of apostasy (*riddah*) and violent martyrdom. Hypocrisy is widespread—especially among Islamophobic liberals whose insistence upon the right to free speech amounts to tolerating only speech of which they approve.

Another clue is the heated confusion continually sparked by the term 'secularism' within the Arabic, Farsi and Turkish language communities. Symptomatic is the absence of a term in Arabic to describe the secular, secularity, or secularism. The word initially chosen for secularism was *dahriyin*, a Qur'anic term used to describe atheists by Jamal-Eddin Al-Afghani in his reply to the attacks on Islam by Ernest Renan. The subsequently preferred neologism *'almaniyyah*, a response to the French term *laïcisme*, first appeared at the end of the nineteenth-century in the dictionary *Muhit Muhit* written by the Christian Lebanese scholar Boutrus al-Bustani. *'Almaniyyah* displayed no verb root—*'almana*, the word for 'secularise', doesn't exist—and was instead derived from *'alam* (world) because its literal translation, *'la diniyah* (non-religious) would have been rejected outright by Muslims, for whom (according to the principle *al-Islam din wa-dawlah*) the division between the temporal and the spiritual is literally unthinkable.

The word 'secularism' subsequently became an insult in the ears of many Muslims. The reasons were more than etymological. Secular Europeans—supposedly open to the world and open to openness itself—normally harboured anti-Muslim prejudices. Indeed, the whole history of secularism as a normative ideal has been weighed down by outright hostility to Muslims, whose roots are old and deep in the European region. When read from the standpoint of the limits of secularism, books such as Maxime Rodinson's *La fascination de l'Islam* (1980), Norman Daniel's *Islam and the West: The Making of an Image* (1960), R. W. Southern's *Western Views of Islam in the Middle Ages* (1962), and Albert Hourani's *Islam in European Thought* (1991), are disturbing. They illustrate with numerous examples how the new-fangled doctrine of secularism in fact carried over virtually unchallenged anti-Muslim prejudices that stemmed back to the times when the Christian countries of the West first perceived the newly converted Saracens, or Arabs, as little better than a plague, like so many other barbarian groups.

The birth of the ideals of European unity and peace, fed by Latin Christendom's gradually developing ideological unity and battles against Islam in Spain, southern Italy, Sicily, and in the Holy Land during the eleventh century, combined to transform and sharpen the random prejudice into a principled hostility to Muslims. The ideology of anti-Islam was supplemented with efforts, initiated by twelfth-century Latin authors, to give free rein to 'the ignorance of triumphant imagination' (R. W. Southern) by describing Muhammad as a sorcerer whose magic and deceit had destroyed the Church in Africa and the East. Religious polemics drawing upon fabulous tales, designed to titillate popular taste, were directed toward imaginary Muslims, easily eliminated on paper. Others simply viewed the Muslim world as a veritable spring of luxury goods—ivory, precious fabrics, spices, papyrus, olive oil—and as a market for tar, slaves, furs, fabrics, swords, wood and iron—all to be exploited for Christian benefit, by violence or stealth.

Then there were those good Christian appeasers, Wolfram von Eschenbach for example, who appealed for an end to the hatred towards pagans (Muslims), who are as they are, he claimed, only because they have not yet had the privilege of hearing Christ's message—a claim reminiscent of the latter-day Ulster Presbyterian moralising about the need for Zionists and Palestinians to make peace by embracing Jesus Christ. A variation on this theme was the call (by the English theologian John Wycliffe, for example) to reform the Christian Church by returning to the purity of pristine Christianity—which would be enough to bring Islam, itself a schism, a kind of dangerous perversion of Christianity, to its knees.

With the advance of the Ottoman Empire into the Balkan region of Christian Europe the old campaigns against infidels became a defence against the sinister, barbarian 'Turk' (*bellum contra barbaros*, as it was often called at the time), who was seen to be inspired by a virulent hatred of 'Civilization'. Sometimes the noted achievements of the Ottomans (e.g., their tolerance toward all sorts of religious minorities) softened prejudices into ambivalence. A case in point was Voltaire's vacillation between a defence of Mohammad as a profound political thinker and founder of a rational religion, and his scathing attack on Mohammad as the prototype of all the impostors who have enslaved souls by resorting to religious fables. There were also many Christian experiments in living peacefully with Muslims, some of which— like the Christian sacrifice of sheep at the shrines of Muslim saints and the praying of Muslims in Christian churches in Syria—have survived until today. There were also occasions when curiosity about Islam turned into exoticism, that is, the thrill of being transported, through stories and representations, without ever leaving Christian Europe, into another world, essentially exotic and picturesque, a nonexistent phantasmagoria wherein fantastic genies could do good or evil, at their whim, a world of gaudy colours and magnificent fabrics, of veiled women at the disposal of men who dined while seated on mats, of palaces decorated with gold, silver and marble, a world whose growing poverty seemed only to add to its charm, sealed off from the rest of the world in its own specificity.

This European fascination with Islam was usually ungenerous, and sometimes murderous. Throughout modern times, there were numerous restatements and variations on the theme of the satanism of Islam—the very word itself suggesting domination, violence, ignorance, fanaticism, misogyny, international conspiracy. Today's 'secular' hostility towards Islam can be seen as a restatement and variation on the old theme of the satanism of Islam. Such hostility helps explain why most contemporary Muslim scholars mistrust or reject outright the ideal of secularism. 'Secularism is Satan imitating God', the leading Turkish Islamist Ali Bulaç has remarked.[17] He echoes the widespread impression that European talk of secularity is hubris, that it has always been a cover for hypocrites who think Muslims can progress only by following the path marked out by the West, which includes the renunciation of religion.

Some Islamist scholars, Muhammad Mahdi Shams al-din and Rachid al-Ghannouchi for instance, acknowledge that in the European context the doctrine of secularism helped to tame Christian fundamentalism and to nurture the values of civility and powersharing.[18] There are others, like Abdolkarim Soroush and Abdou Filali-Ansary, who point out that Muslim societies—including contemporary Iran—have always had strongly endogenous capacities for institutionalising secular or 'this-worldly' forms of life.[19] But these scholars are agreed that the attempted western secularisation of the twentieth-century Muslim world has produced dictatorship, state-enforced religion, the violation of human and civil rights and the weakening or outright destruction of civil society. In a word, secularity has won a reputation for humiliating Muslims—humiliating them through the exercise of Western double standards in Kuwait, Algeria and Palestine, through the corrupt despotism of comprador governments, and through the permanent threat of being crushed by the economic, technological, political, cultural, and military might of the American-led West.

The militant Islamic rejection of secularism within the geographical crescent stretching from Morocco to Mindanao understandably worries many in the West. The material stakes are high and the concern that anti-secularism will prove to be a cover for brutal power-grabbing, instead of benign power-sharing, remains poignant, largely untested by events. Anxiety centres on Hama–the name of a town in Syria which is remembered with much unspoken fear, a terrifying symbol of what happens when the armed forces of secularism drown their throat-slitting opponents in a bloodbath. For citizens living in the old democracies, such conflict should serve as a reminder that secularism shelters violent intolerance and, more generally, that we live in times marked by religious protest, the return of the sacred, and the general desecularisation of political and social life.

It is strange that so few scholars—Reinhold Bernhardt, Gilles Keppel and Ronald Thiemann are notable recent exceptions—are reflecting imaginatively on these trends. Public ignorance or outright denial of their significance, especially by hardline secularists, is also widespread. But here and there can be found pockets of genuine public unease about the cramping effects of secularism. There are calls for a new political philosophy which is rid of fictions about the withering away and privatisation of religion. And within NGO and government circles and courts of law, there are practical efforts to fashion new policy compromises—such as employers' provision for festive and prayer times, believers' exemptions from certain civil laws, the admission of Muslim schools into the state-subsidised voluntary-aided sector in Britain—which seek to accommodate better the preferences of non-believers and believers alike.

These developments prompt many questions. Is the nineteenth-century doctrine of secularism, still cherished by most democrats a century later—including liberals who appeal for the wholesale removal of religion from the political agenda—in fact a conflict-producing ideology that threatens the free-thinking pluralism of democracy as we currently experience it? For the sake of a more democratic future, ought this ideal be jettisoned? If so, does that imply that the inherited secularist categories of church and state, together with the corresponding notion of their 'separation', need to be abandoned, if only because the terms 'church' and 'state' are insufficiently complex to deal with the growing diversity of religious practices and governmental regula-tions of morality? Should we stop searching for universal principles, like secularism, through which to regard religion? Must we instead give priority to context-bound judgments that recognise that all morality—including all religious discourse and that of its secular opponents—arises in particular contexts?

Other questions become pertinent. For instance: should we not recognise, in public controversies about the 'truth' of religion versus the 'truth' of secularism that the Law of Never-Ending Argument applies: that we can't be absolutely sure that God exists, or does not exist; that when we talk about God we don't know for certain who or what we are talking about; and that, conversely, we don't know how best to summarise, using the language of immanence, the true nature of Humanity and the World? Does this Law of Never-Ending Argument compel us to see that the secularist view that religious believers are like Ixion copulating with clouds and breeding monsters applies equally to secularists, and that therefore new desecularised compromises between non-believers and believers are now required? Are we thus left with no other political option but to seek new ways of maximising the freedom and equality and mutual respect of non-believers and believers alike—with special emphasis being given to those who currently suffer the injustices produced by a nineteenth-century doctrine whose universalist pretensions are no longer credible?

Notes

1 Peter Brown, *Authority and the Sacred. Aspects of the Christianisation of the Roman World*, Cambridge, Cambridge University Press, 1995, especially part 1.
2 Charles Taylor, 'Modes of Secularism' in Rajeev Bhargava, ed., *Secularism and its Critics*, Calcutta, Oxford University Press, 1998, pp. 31–53.
3 Peter Berger, *The Sacred Canopy: Elements of a Sociological Theory of Religion*, New York, Garden City, 1969, p. 108.
4 *ibid.*, p. 127.

5 Hermann Luebbe, *Saekularisierung—Geschichte eines ideenpolitischen Begriffs*, Freiburg, 1965.
6 See, for example, Ludwig Feuerbach, 'Preliminary Theses on the Reform of Philosophy' in *The Fiery Brook: Selected Writings of Ludwig Feuerbach*, New York, Garden City, 1972, pp. 153–73.
7 William Edward Hartpole Lecky, London, 1890, volume 2, chapter 5.
8 Samuel P. Huntington, *The Clash of Civilizations and the Remaking of World Order*, New York & London, Simon & Schuster, 1996.
9 Alan D. Gilbert, 'Secularization and the Future', in Sheridan Gilley and W. J. Sheils, eds., *A History of Religion in Britain. Practice and Belief from Pre-Roman Times to the Present*, Cambridge, MA. & Oxford, 1994, pp. 512–3.
10 Charles Taylor, *Philosophical Arguments*, Cambridge, MA & London, Harvard University Press, 1995, chapter 13.
11 Richard Rorty, 'Religion as a Conversation-Stopper', privately circulated manuscript.
12 A well-known American example of this line of argument is Stephen L. Carter, *The Culture of Disbelief: How American Law and Politics Trivialize Religious Devotion*, New York, Doubleday, 1993.
13 Hannah Arendt, 'Religion and the Intellectuals', *Partisan Review* 17, February 1950, p. 114.
14 See John Keane, *Civil Society: Old Images, New Visions*, Cambridge, Polity Press, 1998, especially pp. 147–8.
15 See John Keane, *Václav Havel: A Political Tragedy in Six Acts*, London, Bloomsbury, 1999, pp. 438–47.
16 'Laïcité', a public lecture delivered at the University of London (31 May 1996). On the Turkish case, see Stanford J. Shaw and Ezel Kural Shaw, *History of the Ottoman Empire and Modern Turkey*, volume 2, New York and London, 1977, chapter 6. The French case is analysed in Jean Bauberot, 'The Two Thresholds of Laïcization' in Rajeev Bhargava, ed., *op. cit.*, pp. 94–136; and John Keane, *Tom Paine: a Political Life*, London, Bloomsbury, 1995, p. 389–400.
17 Interview with Ali Bulaç, Istanbul (30 March 1996).
18 Interview with Muhammad Mahdi Shams al-din, Beirut (3 April 1996); and my discussion of the political thinking of Rachid al-Ghannouchi in *Civil Society: Old Images, New Visions, op. cit.*, pp. 28–31.
19 Interview with Abdolkarim Soroush, Tehran (18 October 1999); Abdou Filali-Ansary, 'The Debate on Secularism in Contemporary Societies of Muslims', *International Institute for the Study of Islam in the Modern World Newsletter*, 2, March 1999, p. 6.

Living with Difference in India

SUSANNE HOEBER RUDOLPH AND LLOYD I. RUDOLPH

Legal Pluralism and Legal Universalism in Historical Context

Modern India has provided a setting for the contest between legal pluralism and legal universalism. Legal pluralism recognises and legitimises the personal law of India's religious communities. Legal universalism engenders calls for a uniform civil code. By modern India, we mean the India of the East India Company [c1757–1857], the British raj [1858–1947], Congress nationalism [1885–1947] and independent India [1947-present]. We will visit times, places and events in search of discourses and practices that shaped legal recognition of personal law and the debate over instituting a uniform civil code.

In particular, we will visit the context, mainly in Bengal but in memory and discourse standing for 'India', between the particularistic Orientalists and the universalistic Utilitarians during the East India Company era; the trauma of the 1857 rebellion and its aftermath, Queen Victoria's 1858 Proclamation accepting difference; the fracture of partition as it was foreshadowed in Sir Sayyad Ahmed Khan's 'many nations' doctrine; Mohammed Ali Jinnah's two nation doctrine; the Indian National Congress' universalist one nation doctrine; the cohabitation in Congress' secularism between equal recognition of all religions and special privileging of minority religion, particularly Islam; and the rise (and faltering?) of the Hindu nationalist ideology of homogeneity in the 1980s.

Legal pluralism has been one way to give expression to India's continuously and variously constructed multicultural society. Legal universalism has been associated with liberal and nationalist ideas about equal, uniform citizenship. Speaking analytically, legal pluralism posits corporate groups as the basic units, the building blocks, of a multi-cultural society and state. Particular legal rights and obligations attach to collective identities such as Hindu, Muslim, Christian, Sikh, Jain, Buddhist and Parsi, and to *sampradayas* [sects] and *quoms* [communities] such as Dadupanthis, Kabirpanthis, Sunnis, Shias, etc. Legal universalism treats individuals as the basic unit of society and the state and imagines homogeneous citizens with uniform legal rights and obligations.

Indian law and politics have vacillated between these two positions. The Supreme Court in a landmark case, *Balaji v State of Mysore* [1963], tried to quantify the proportionate weight that should be accorded to each. The case involved group rights in the form of quotas in university admissions and government jobs for Dalits [ex-untouchables] and for OBCs [other backward classes, an administrative euphemism for lower castes]. Article 16[4] of the constitution on the one hand guarantees the 'equality of opportunity in matters of public employment'. On the other hand, it provides that

nothing in this article shall prevent the State from making any provision for the reservation of appointments or posts in favour of any backward class of citizens which, in the opinion of the State, is not adequately represented in the services under the State.

The Court split the difference; it limited permissible reservations to 49 per cent. Beyond 49 per cent the Court held would be a *fraud on the constitution* because it would impinge upon the constitutional mandates providing for equality before the law [Article 14] and prohibiting discrimination [Article 15]. In other words, *Balaji* in 1963 weighted legal pluralism in the form of group rights at 49 per cent and legal universalism in the form of equal citizenship at 51 per cent.

The institutional progenitors and philosophical lineages of legal pluralism and legal universalism were differentially mobilized and reinforced by Company, colonial, nationalist and post-colonial political actors. The rise of Hindu nationalism and the articulation of an *hindutva* [*Hinduness*] ideology in the 1980s and 1990s, lent new meanings and urgency to the tension between pluralism and universalism. The tension is likely to continue for the foreseeable future in a multi-cultural society and state that has to accommodate on a daily basis the contrasting imperatives of integration and diversity. Neither is likely to drive out the other.

Legal pluralism is not simply a question of values. It is also a question of power, of who gets what when and where. 'Universality' in the law is not only valued by enlightenment liberals and Fabian socialists, it is also the strategy of centralizing modern states. Pluralism in the law is both a norm and the strategy of those who favour dividing, limiting and sharing sovereignty in federal and pluralist states that allow for diversified geographically and culturally defined communities.

The Company Discovers and Legitimizes Difference; Cultural Federalism and Legal Pluralism

Cultural federalism is a term we have coined to suggest that India has dealt with diversity in ways that recognise legal identities on the basis of cultural as well as territorial boundaries. The Ottoman millet 'system', under which leaders of the Greek Orthodox and of Christian, Armenian, Jewish and other communities were given civil as well as religious authority over their respective flocks represents a significant historical example of cultural federalism. As we shall see, early East India Company doctrine and practice followed similar principles. In independent India, cultural federalism is given expression in Article 29 of the Constitution, what might be called the multi-cultural clause, which protects the interests of minorities by granting them the right to 'conserve' their 'language, script and culture,' and Article 30 which gives minorities the 'right to establish and administer educational institutions.' These provisions are in tension with the universalistic proposals of Article 44, a non-justiciable Directive Principles of State Policy that enjoins the state to 'endeavor to secure for the citizens a uniform civil code throughout the territory of India.'

So why did Warren Hastings, who in 1774 became the East India Company's first Governor-General; Sir William Jones, a Company judge in Bengal and one of the first Englishmen to master Sanskrit; and the stellar scholars, also servants of the Company, who comprised the founding generations of the Asiatic Society of Bengal, adopt a policy of cultural federalism and legal pluralism? Why did they decide to apply 'the laws of the Koran with respect to Mohammedans and that of the Shaster with respect to Hindus'? Why did Jones construct a world composed of Hindus and Muslims? Why and how did he construct the categories 'Hindu' and 'Muslim,' categories that, in changing guises and with changing meanings and consequences, are present today at the close of the twentieth century?

A post-colonial perspective leads to reading 19th and 20th century categories and outcomes into the mentalities and intentions of 18th century actors. The motive becomes imperial power, the tactic religious division. Power becomes as un-nuanced a determinant of thought as control of the means of production.

We read the ideas and actions of Hastings and his Asiatic Society colleagues, including their construction of Hindu and Mohammedan, as shaped by two concerns: the sources and meaning of 'civilization' conceived of within the framework 18th century European understandings of world history; and, for Hastings in particular, a powerful sense of being a *local* ruler. Hastings Jones and their Asiatic Society colleagues, all trained in European classical traditions, developed a 'civilizational eye.' It came to understand legal pluralism in terms of large, coherent cultural wholes defined by great languages and their classical texts. In their cultural imaginations, Hastings and Jones treated Sanskritic and Persian civilizations as equivalent to those of Greece and Rome. Their sense of being local rulers led them to do what they thought local rulers did, rely on the laws of the peoples under their authority to administer justice. Anachronistic efforts to read divide and rule communal politics into Company policy need to be modified by attention to the civilizational perspective and the self-understanding of Company servants as local rulers.

English 18th century representatives of the East India Company acted as agents of the Mughal emperor. At least nominally they understood themselves as agents, not principals. At this state of the British relationship to India, their mentality, as Uday Mehta, writing about 'liberalism and empire' might have put it, was more Burkean than Lockean, more attuned to pluralist multiculturalism than to liberal universalism. Hence they recognised and accepted the existence and value of different civilisations on the Indian subcontinent. A 'Burkean' consciousness accounts for what we characterise as Warren Hastings' policy of cultural federalism, a policy which made each group subject to its own laws. In a much quoted memorandum Hastings ordered that

in all suits regarding inheritance, marriage, caste and other religious usages and institutions, the laws of the Koran with respect to the Mahomedans and those of the shaster with respect to the Gentoos [Hindus] shall be invariably adhered to; on all such occasions the Moulvies or Brahmins shall respectively attend to expound the law, and they shall sign the report and assist in passing the decree.[1]

Recent scholarship on the 18th century questions the Company's emphasis in the Hastings era on religious and caste groups to construct Indian society. The result entrenched the categories, religion and caste, in the mentalities and practices of succeeding generations. For the purposes of our argument, which groups are featured is less important than the fact that self-regulating groups with cultural markings rather than unmarked standardised individuals were thought to constitute society.

An Indian Theory of Self-Regulating Groups

Henry Thomas Colebrooke, leader of the second generation of Asiatic Society of Bengal Orientalists, distinguished Sanskritist, author of *Digest of Hindu Law* [1798] and founder of the Royal Asiatic Society, joined other scholars in the belief that in India the laws of groups pre-existed the state. He cites an injunction from Bhrigu, a mythical law giver, that calls on each category of person to litigate controversies according to its own law:

The frequenters of forests should cause their differences to be determined by one of their own order; members of a society, by persons belonging to that society; people appertaining to an army, by such as belong to the army . . . husbandmen, mechanics, artists . . . robbers or irregular soldiers, should adjust their controversies according to their own particular laws.

Sanskrit law texts held that the king should oversee the self-regulating society rather than create laws for society. The *Manusmriti*, initially translated from Sanskrit into English by Sir William Jones, holds that 'the king [was] created as the protector of the classes and the stages of life, that are appointed each to its own particular duty, in proper order.' Nor were such injunctions found solely in the Hindu texts favoured by the early British Orientalists such as Jones and Henry Thomas Colebrooke. Richard Eaton shows us numerous exemplars of legal understandings in 16th century, Mughal-ruled Bengal, where Muslim administrators enforced laws particular to specific communities. Such an understanding of Indian society supported the view that Indian society was constituted by groups.

SUSANNE HOEBER RUDOLPH AND LLOYD RUDOLPH

Legal Uniformity and Individual Rights Enter the Contest

Group concepts flourished under Company rule as long as Jones and his Orientalist brethren held sway. Their view of the value of Indian civilizations and social formations and practices was challenged and largely overturned with the arrival in 1828 of Lord William Bentinck, the first of a series of liberal and utilitarian Governor Generals. Liberal individualist themes now competed with earlier Orientalist constructions of India as a society constituted of groups. Liberal utilitarians in the era of Bentinck and Macauley strove to liberate Indians from domination by groups, to unravel individuals from the grip of family, caste and religious community, to strengthen individual choice against collective decision. Until Victoria's 1858 proclamation reversed its course, the Benthamite thrust posited that individualism and universalism were a requirement for progress and civilized living.

It was Governor General Dalhousie's egalitarian policy of 'treating all natives in much the same manner' that helped bring on the 1857 rebellion.[2] Corporate structures, James Fitzjames Stephen observed, would 'decay because they represent a crude form of socialism, paralyzing the individual energy and inconsistent with the fundamental principles of our rule.' A series of legislative acts, none of them very consequential outside a small circle of urban-based cosmopolitan elites, advanced this individualist vision. Several were designed to establish rights independent of the joint family, the customary holder of property: the Freedom of Religion Act of 1850 saved converts, upon conversion, from losing their identity as Hindus, an identity they needed to secure property rights in the joint family; the Widow Remarriage Act of 1856 asserted a woman's rights in the face of customary demands of the joint family in many upper castes; the Gains of Learning Act made it possible for a son educated by his joint family to appropriate the subsequent income to himself instead of having to share it with the family. The introduction of wills substituted choice, by means of a legal instrument, for the prescriptive claims of the joint family.

Individualism and legal universalism gained a formidable ally when in 1835 Thomas Babbington Macaulay joined Bentinck's government as law member of the council. Macaulay, who unashamedly admitted having 'no knowledge of either Sanskrit or Arabic,' alleged in a rightly notorious passage

that all the historical information which has been collected from all the books written in the Sanskrit language is less valuable than what may be found in the most paltry abridgements used at preparatory schools in England.

He wrote a minute on education that convinced a majority of Bentinck's Council to overturn the Orientalist support for Indian learning and languages. Macaulay's vision was to assimilate all mankind into the higher civilization of the educated Victorian. His goal was to form 'a class of persons, Indian in blood and colour, but English in taste, in opinions, in morals, and in intellect' (Wolpert, *op. cit.*, p 215). In 1835 Bentinck's Council agreed to allocate its educational funds to teaching western learning to young Indians in the English language. Macaulay's project of Anglicized uniformity was deepened in 1857 when Sir Charles Wood's 1854 Education Despatch recommending *inter alia* the establishment of English medium universities in the three presidencies—Bengal, Madras and Bombay—was acted upon. By 1885 English higher education had produced a national Indian elite who had 'studied the classics of English literature and . . . followed . . . the course of politics in Europe [including] the rise of nationalism . . .'[3] They were on the road to liberal universalism. In 1885 72 of them met in Bombay to form the Indian National Congress. They imagined, or most of them did, that India would be a nation, constituted by individuals acting on majoritarian principles.

The Reaction Against Liberal Universalism

A new discourse began after the 1857 revolt. The revolt had destroyed British confidence: loss of control, not only military but also cultural, was unexpected and sudden. 'Henceforth, the British in India would always walk in fear . . . now the British stepped back permanently into their neat little compound, fenced and right-angled, of facts and rules'.[4]

Queen Victoria's 1858 proclamation repudiated and reversed the utilitarian and evangelical inspired liberal universalism of Company policy, a policy that extended from Bentinck and Macaulay in the 1830s through Dalhousie in the 1850s. But the retreat functioned to moderate rather than eliminate the processes of rationalisation and universalisation already set in motion.

Non-intervention was thought an appropriate remedy for the causes believed to have led to the 1857 revolt, utilitarian and evangelical inspired 'reforms' and 'annexations' under the doctrine of 'lapse'.[5] The Queen, who in 1877 was made Queen-Empress of the British empire in India, pledged to respect and protect India's alien diversity, including its religious practices. The proclamation declared 'it to be our royal will and pleasure that none be in anywise favoured, none molested or disquieted, by reason of their religious faith or observances, but that all shall alike enjoy the equal and impartial protection of the law; and we do strictly charge and enjoin all those who may be in authority under us that they abstain from all interference with religious belief or worship of any of our subjects on pain of our highest displeasure.' (Wolpert, *op. cit.*, pp 240–1.)

Queen Victoria's 1858 non-interference proclamation was, of course, a doctrine, not a practice. Gordon Johnson argues that Henry Maine's cautious, conservative approach to legal reform can be taken to epitomize the way post-1858 British rule in India managed change while pursuing a doctrine of non-intervention.

As Law Member [1862–69], Maine passed no striking laws . . . Although . . . responsible for over two hundred separate Acts, his colleagues are remarkably unanimous in their welcome of his low key approach. Sir Richard Strachey found that Maine's virtue law in that 'he limited itself to the actual requirements of his time' while Courtney Ilbert . . . praised Maine for abstaining 'from passing a great many measures of doubtful utility'. Here was no adventurous law-giver as Macaulay had been thirty years before . . .'[6]

While Maine was nominally complying with the non-intervention order, his Acts

gave legislative form to civil usages and religious practices of particular groups of Indians, and here, while there were some notable exceptions as regards marriage, the overall tendency was to put into statute form customary laws and to do so in ways which were prevalent at the time . . .

The effect of his tinkering was to universalise and standardise the law's relationship to society, and to move legal pluralism outward and upward from the diversely constituted periphery toward a more uniform national level. It set the stage for the struggle in the 1990s between minority rights based on legal pluralism and the various perceived requirements of the Directive Principle's Article 44 'to secure a uniform civil code for the citizens' of India. Victoria's retreat from the utilitarians' efforts to rationalise Indian administration and to codify Indian law, left Indian society with a viable group life, but stood in tension with an incompatible universalising discourse.

Group Rights as Defence Against Majoritarianism

Sir Sayyid Ahmad Khan, the pre-eminent Muslim modernist reformer, contributed mightily to the British resurrection of a corporate theory of Indian society. He found the formal creation of Indian nationalism in 1885 by anglicised liberal universalists a threat and a challenge. From his perspective, Muslims had much to fear from claims that there was *an* Indian nation. Few Muslims had responded to Macauley's call to become 'English in taste, in opinions, in morals, and in intellect,' or to Sir Charles Wood's call to be educated in English language learning. Sir Sayyid typified the ambivalence of his time as he encouraged Muslims to join Anglo-Victorian universalism on the one hand, while creating a protective arena for Muslim group rights on the other.

Muslim 'backwardness' had many causes, one of which was that the British, having wrested power from the Mughals in whose name the East India Company had ruled India, feared and distrusted (even while emulating) their former Muslim masters. The 1858 rebellion was in part an effort by Indian Muslims and others to oust the British and to place Bahadur Shah II, a Mughal emperor, back on the throne. Sir Sayyid tried to deal with a debilitating psychology of past greatness and with the nostalgia and inertia that marked the downward mobility of Muslim lineages and families who remembered being the rulers of India. His goal was 'to lure his community from its tents of Perso-Arabic mourning for the demise of Mughal glory into the market place of vigorous competition with Hindus, Parsis, Christians for ICS (Indian Civil Service) positions and the privileges of Anglo-Indian Power.' (Wolpert, *op. cit.*, p 264.)

To that end in 1875, on Queen Victoria's birthday, two years before she was declared Queen-Empress of India, Sir Sayyid established the Muhammadan Anglo-Oriental College at Aligarh. The young Tory from Cambridge who became M.A.O.'s second principal, Theodore Beck, modelled it on the British Public School: games, little magazines, a liberal curriculum. Sir Sayyid hoped to create an alternative anglicized elite that could hold its ground with, even best, the elite that Macaulay's and Woods' educational reforms had brought into being. By gaining positions in the ICS, the 'steel frame' that governed India for the British crown, Muslims, too, would have seats at the table.

Sir Sayyid found it difficult to accept Congress' one nation theory. For him India was 'inhabited by different nationalities.' In 1883 in a debate in the Governor-General's Council on the Central Provinces (now Madhya Pradesh) Local Self Government Bill, he warned the Council that

in borrowing from England the system of representative institutions, it is of the greatest importance to remember the socio-political matters in which India is distinguishable from England . . . India . . . is inhabited by vast populations of different races and creeds . . . The community of race and creed makes the people one and the same nation . . . the whole of England forms but one community . . . in India . . . there is no fusion of the various races . . . religious distinctions are still violent . . . education in its modern sense has not made an equal or proportionate progress among all sections of the people . . . . So long as . . . (such) differences form an important element in the socio-political life of the country, the system of election, pure and simple (i.e. majority rule), cannot be adopted.

Without a homogeneous nation, and India for the foreseeable future, in Sir Sayyid's view, could not be a homogeneous nation, safeguards such as reserved seats, separate electorates, 'weightage,' and nominated members were necessary to insure that 'due and just balance in the representation of the various sections of the Indian population . . . .' (Coupland, *op. cit.*, pp 155–6.)

Muhammad Ali Jinnah, the father of Pakistan and its Qaid-i-Azam (great leader), was a figurative son of Aligarh, i.e. the kind of anglicized, modern Muslim that Sir Sayyid Ahmad Khan sought to create. Like Sir Sayyid he, too, prospered under British policy and rule. And he, too, fearing a Hindu majority, searched for mechanisms that would allow a Muslim community to have its fair share of seats in the chambers of government. Sir Sayyid had spoken of 'many nations;' in 1937 Jinnah began speaking of two, Pakistan and India. With partition into two successor states in 1947, 10 per cent (35 million then, 110 million now) of India's population were Muslims. How, without raj-like safeguards, was the new state to recognise and legitimate difference and protect minority rights in a parliamentary democracy with universal suffrage and majority rule?

SUSANNE HOEBER RUDOLPH AND LLOYD RUDOLPH

Communal Reservation as Group Entitlement

In pre-independence India, the answer to the question, how to reconcile minority rights with majority rule, was communal reservations. Until the second half of the nineteenth century, the colonial government's policy had expressed the group principle mainly through legal practice in the arena of personal law. As representation of Indians was timidly and haltingly introduced into local and provincial governments in the 1880s, the principle took on political form. If India consisted of groups, groups would be the basis of representation.

The political expression of this vision was a policy of legislative reservations that emphasised the group nature of Indian society. From the first inclusion of Indians in governing councils at the state and national level after 1858, corporatist principles dictated the units: landowners, university bodies, municipalities, and eventually minority religious entities—Muslims, Christians, Sikhs. (See Coupland, *op. cit.*, vol. 1, pp. 47, 128, 134, 151.) In the South, the battle over representation took a different form. Because indigenous resistance to Brahmanic dominance surfaced early in the 20th century, caste rather than religious community became the contested group identity in politics and bureaucracy. The British introduced reservations for 'forward' and 'backward' non-Brahman castes into legislatures, civil services and educational institutions in South India beginning in the second decade of the twentieth century.[7]

The most important embodiment of the group principle before independence was a scheme to give 'safeguards' to minority religious communities by providing them with separate electorates and reserved seats. By privileging these categories for purposes of representation, the British shaped as much as they reflected the idea that religious identities trumped all others. In the process they invented the principle that religious groups were homogeneous. Separate electorates had the effect of deterring appeals to cross-cutting cleavages, appeals which might allow individuals to escape corporatist domination and isolation. First institutionalised in the Morley-Minto constitutional reforms of 1909, reservations based on religious community, i.e. for Muslims, continued in the Montagu-Chelmsford reforms of 1919 and in the constitutional framework created by the Government of India Act of 1935.

Nationalists regarded 'safeguards' which included both reservations of seats and 'weightage,' extra seats for minorities, as a policy designed to divide and rule Indians. The principle spread. During the negotiations preceding the Government of 1935 India Acts, untouchables lobbied for similar group recognition, for separate electorates and reservations. They succeeded in having seats reserved for untouchables but failed to gain separate electorates after Gandhi's 1932 'fast unto death' against what he regarded as a British scheme to divide and weaken nationalism. The potential for divisiveness of group reservations was realised in 1947, when India at independence was partitioned into two successor states, India and Pakistan.

The idea of group protection also infiltrated nationalist policy and practice. Paradoxically, it was the nationalist faction most wedded to equal citizenship grounded in territorially organised individuals, the rationalist modernists allied with Jawaharlal Nehru, who encouraged a decision rule within the Congress party and in Congress-controlled legislatures that gave groups the right to veto decisions affecting their interests. The rule was first adopted in the Congress party's constitution, then incorporated in the Lucknow pact of 1916, which for a time united the Indian National Congress and the Muslim League on nationalist objectives. The rule provided that if three-quarters of the minority community, i.e. Muslim members, opposed a policy deemed to affect their interests, the policy could not go forward. The decision-rule recognised the limits on majority rule in democracies. Minorities can threaten exit if denied voice.[8]

Between Group Identity and Individual Rights: The Constituent Assembly

We have tried to show how at independence in 1947 India's constitution makers had available alternative and competing norms stressing group particularism on the one hand and individualist universalism on the other. Historical processes and events had endowed these concepts with changing meanings and consequences over time. Independence in 1947 and the constituent assembly that sat until 1950 provided the high water mark of liberal universalism. Since then, with the powerful exception of the rise of Hindu nationalism in the 1980s, difference and group identity expressed in the legitimation of legal pluralism, multi-cultural ideology and minority rights have gained ground.

In 1947, nationalist opinion held that group-based norms and practices, such as separate electorates, reserved seats and weightage, found in British efforts to bring representative government to India in the reform acts of 1909, 1919, and 1935, were responsible for the partition of the sub-continent. The nationalists who ran the constituent assembly were likely to be socialists like Nehru, pluralist inclusivists like Gandhi, or liberal constructivists like Sapru and Rau, not primordialists or essentialists like raj officials or Hindu nationalist and Muslim nationalist politicians. Many nationalists believed that the religious and caste categories found in British censuses and official discourse and law were not natural or primordial, but the products of the raj's historical circumstance and fertile imaginations. The incentives offered by officially created groups and the reservations extended to them inhibited appeals to cross-cutting cleavages, and cemented solidarities based on religion and caste. The many other identities and interests active and available on the sub-continent were marginalized by official raj sociology.

The Nehruvians, who were hegemonic in the Congress party and in the constituent assembly, were doggedly determined to deny that religious identities trumped all others, and to see to it that individual rights and citizen equality prevail. They say to it that provisions of the 1935 Government of India Act, which served as the basic text for the new constitution, were purged of provisions recognising and privileging group identity. Reserved seats and separate electorates for Muslims, Sikhs, Christians and other minorities were eliminated. The only exception to the elimination of group rights was reservations by proportion of the population for the scheduled castes [ex-untouchables] and tribes.

After independence, partition and the departure of the British on August 15, 1947, the remaining Muslim members in the constituent assembly were uncertain about what to expect and what course to follow. Sixty per cent of unpartitioned India's Muslims were now in Pakistan. Did the greater vulnerability of the remainder require the continuation, even the strengthening, of minority safeguards, or did it suggest ingratiating themselves with Congress leaders by offering to surrender them? Vallabhbhai Patel, the Deputy Prime Minister and Home and States Minister, who in retrospect appears as a Hindu nationalist, 'quietly and privately put a great deal of pressure on the minorities to relinquish special privileges' but 'was too considerate of minority fears—and too much the strategist—to force the issue . . . . (Publicly he said that) the giving up of reservation should not be forced on any minority.' 'The (Muslim) community,' Granville Austin tells us, 'was deeply split by the issue. Ultimately it would decide . . . to forego even reservations in the Legislature, hoping by its sacrifice to ensure fair treatment from the Hindu majority.'[9]

It was not until May 1949 that the constituent assembly took its final decisions on the reservation of seats in legislatures. H. C. Mookerjee was a Christian member who, unlike others of his community in the constituent assembly, believed that minorities, his own and others, should voluntarily give up reservations. It was Mookerjee who, on behalf of the relevant Advisory Committee, moved the resolution to abolish reservations for minorities. Scheduled castes and tribes were spared. All that minorities need, he urged, for protection from democratic majorities re the fundamental rights guaranteed to all citizens in Part III of the constitution. Its articles 14 through 29 provide *inter alia* for equality under the law, prohibiting discrimination, protecting freedom of speech, life and personal liberty, and guaranteeing freedom of conscience and freedom to profess, practise and propagate religion.

Mookerjee urged minorities to stop thinking in terms of sub-national minority groups. 'I have all along held,' he said, 'that India is one nation.' His resolution carried 'with nearly everyone present agreeing or saying they did.' (Austin, *op. cit.*)

Partition had taught not one, but two lessons. One was that minority safeguards, particularly reservations, can harden cleavages that lead to secession, the other, that the Muslims in partitioned India would continue to feel endangered by what many perceived as a Hindu majority. They needed reassurance that their corporate identity was recognised and that their corporate life secure. The second lesson of partition convinced Nehru and those he led in the dominant Congress party that Muslims in partitioned India needed special guarantees. These took the form of allowing the Muslim community to preserve and practise their personal law.

Group Rights for Lower Castes

Looking back on the era of partition and constitution-making from the perspective of the ideological excitement and political competition of the 1980s and 1990s, two kinds of groups continue to support legal pluralism against the constitutional injunction to implement legal universalism in a uniform civil code. Those groups are lower castes who seek reservations, and religious communities who seek protection for their personal law.[10]

First, caste. As we have seen, reservations of legislative seats for scheduled castes and tribes survived in articles 330 and 332 of the constitution. These provisions had their progenitors in the British privileging of 'backward' castes, expressed in their protection, via 'communal awards,' of non-Brahmin castes in the South beginning in the 1910s. Positive or protective discrimination on behalf of 'backward classes' that began with the scheduled castes and tribes was extended nationally in the 1990s by wide-ranging reservations on behalf of 'OBCs' (Other Backward Classes, an administrative euphemism for lower castes). Such new expressions of legal pluralism were generated by the horizontal mobilization of lower castes in the countryside, where 75 per cent of India's voting population lives. Their high levels of participation in national and state electoral politics have radically transformed the sociological profile of India's national parliament, state assemblies and their cabinets. The rise of the OBCs first in state and then in national politics has tended to marginalise the upper caste, upper class elites who dominated Congress party politics in the Nehru/Gandhi dynasty era.

A second 'Backward Classes Commission' chaired by B. P. Mandal was established to try to implement what the constitution seemed to promise, reservations for 'Other Backward Classes.' Reporting in 1980, the Mandal Commission presented the country with an anthropological index organised by states specifying 3743 backward castes. These were the castes said to qualify as beneficiaries under the constitutional clauses urging special care for 'backward' citizens. The Commission estimated that backward castes listed in its report constituted 52 per cent of the population. It recommended, however, that only 27 per cent reservation be set aside for the OBCs listed. Reservations totaling 52 per cent when added to the 22.5 per cent already reserved for scheduled castes and tribes would violate the Supreme Court's standard in *Balaji* that reservations totalling more than 50 per cent would be a fraud on the constitution, in part because exceeding 50 per cent would violate the equal rights clauses of the constitution.

Even before the Mandal Commission made its recommendations, many Indian states had already enacted legislation providing reservations in educational institutions and government jobs for 'backwards.' When Prime Minister V. P. Singh's government began to implement the Mandal Commission recommendations in 1990, the BJP withdrew its support from his coalition government and soon after launched a *padyatra* (national pilgrimage) on behalf of *Hindutva* [Hinduness]. There were riots and immolations mainly by disgrunted upper caste, upper class students; the government fell, and a mid-term election followed. In 1991 a Congress government under Prime Minister Narasimha Rao took office. It, too, began cautiously to implement the Mandal Commission's recommendations. Today OBC politics and reservations have been, if not fully normalised, at least accepted as part of the rules of the game. Legal pluralism in the form of reservations for particular lower castes seems well established as the 20th century gives way to the 21st.

Minority Rights for Religious Communities: The Uniform Civil Code

Religious collectivities also claimed exemption from universal rules. Having wiped out reservations of legislative seats on the basis of religion, the constituent assembly proceeded to write Article 29, which guarantees the right to maintain distinct cultures. 'Any section of the citizens of India . . . having a distinct language, script [Gurmukhi was a script used by Sikhs; Urdu by Muslims] or culture [a euphemism for religion] shall have the right to preserve the same.' Article 30 guaranteed the right of religious minorities to establish educational institutions and barred the state, which supports private educational institutions, including religious ones, from discriminating against them. The articles raise the question whether it is constitutionally permissible to have different laws for different groups defined according to religion. Not really, the constituent assembly wanted to say. It almost said it. It almost asserted that a uniform civil code supersede the varieties of personal law. But at the last minute, it held its hand.

At the urging of 'liberals' such as Minoo Masani, Amrit Kaur and Hansa Mehta, the constituent assembly considered including a uniform civil code in the justiciable provisions of the constitution. Such a code, embodying general laws applicable to all individuals regardless of religion, would have been mandated to come into force over a five to ten year period.[11] By abolishing the differences in personal law it would 'get rid of these watertight compartments' 'which keep the nation divided.' (Austin, *op. cit.*, p. 80.)

The provision died in committee, but was eventually included in the 'Directive Principles of State Policy,' non-justiciable articles (36 through 51) included in Part IV of the constitution. They articulate the imagined social revolution of the Nehruvian nationalist generation. It expresses purposes and goals but creates no rights. The hesitancy to include an actionable UCC in the constitution reflected the concern of the Nehruvian secular nationalists for the sensibilities and needs of India's religious minorities. They wanted to insure that Muslims particularly, but also Sikhs, Christians, Parsis, Jains and others in secular India would not only feel safe but at home. They were to be not only citizens with equal rights, but also members of religious communities whose different cultures and identities would be secure and honoured through the continued existence and viability of their personal law.

The Uniform Civil Code as Historical Process

One way to think about the uniform civil code is as a process that has gone on for over 150 years and has been continually challenged. For much of that period, in the hands of British reformers before independence and nationalist secularists since independence, the tendency appeared to be in the direction of greater homogeneity. Since the 1970s, forces of difference and identity appear to have strengthened the heterogeneity of religiously based personal law.

Homogeneity was served powerfully in the nineteenth and twentieth centuries by three processes: changes in who administered the law; expansion of universal law by processes of codification; the reformation and homogenization of personal law.

First, administration. The British began with a partial commitment to having the law interpreted by Hindu and Muslim religious adepts, attaching pandits and maulvis to their courts. But these indigenous court advisors were dispensed with in 1864. British magistrates or British trained magistrates became the sole executors of personal law, soundlessly introducing principles of evidence and interpretation that smoothed out differences. The hierarchical organisation that links all courts in India into a single system leading today to the Supreme Court also favoured homogeneity. The court *system* was universalised long before the law.

The great wave of legal codification by the British in the nineteenth century swept away the particularities of criminal law (via the Penal Code of 1860), preserving neither Muslim nor Hindu penalties. A series of civil law acts passed between 1865 and 1872 were based mainly on British civil law, exempting, however, the realm of personal law: marriage, divorce, succession, adoption, property, and definition of family.

Finally, the reformation of the personal law itself led toward uniformity within each of the compartments. To assert legally that there is one undifferentiated 'Hindu' and 'Muslim' personal law was itself a significant act of homogenization. The personal law of Hindu lower and upper castes differs markedly, as does law between regions which have different kinship systems. 'Muslims' too is an amalgam of sectarian identities with different rules and practises. When the Shariat Act was passed in 1937 to regularise and rationalise Muslim law, it wiped out the particular personal laws of several Muslim communities that constituted minorities within Indian Islam: the

Khojas and Cutchi Memons of Gujarat and the Muslims of North West Frontier Province, all of whom followed Hindu laws of inheritance, and the Malsan Muslims who follow matriarchal laws of inheritance. (Dhagamwar, *op. cit.*, p 219.)

Just as the practice of the British courts narrowed the number of precepts accepted as Muslim or Muhammadan law, Muslim hierarchical organisation gave a kind of finality to *sharia* which it could not attain when authority was localised and distributed among many *madrasas* as well as individuals.

If we understand the uniform legal code as a historical process instead of a one-time legal enactment, this is the story of the homogenization process. But there is a parallel story of the survival and reassertion of legal pluralism. The sensational 1985 Shah Bano case encapsulates the intense contemporary tension between the uniformity making process and the pluralist counterforce.

Shah Bano, a divorced Muslim woman, sued her husband for maintenance. The court held her entitled to maintenance under article 125 of the Code of Criminal Procedure, which had often been previously invoked, including cases of Muslim women, to prevent female vagrancy by forcing husbands to support wives whom they had divorced. The Supreme Court decision was rooted in cases dating back to the *raj* that had not occasioned Muslim challenge. This point matters, suggesting that the acceptance of the homogenizing process is premised on the trust and distrust prevailing among contesting groups at particular moments in historical time. The decision was welcomed with jubilation by women's groups, and seen as a step in the direction of a uniform civil code. But the Muslim community *in this instance*, at a historical moment that saw a rising spiral of Hindu nationalism, interpreted the court's decision in favor of Shah Bano as violating Muslim personal law, which mandates that when the marriage contract is terminated by divorce, the husband's financial obligations cease and are to be taken up by blood relatives or Muslim religious bodies.[12] Muslim protests and electoral reaction were sufficiently strong that the Rajiv Gandhi government, which had originally welcomed the decision, reversed course and passed legislation protecting the Muslim personal law in cases of Muslim divorce.

The Shah Bano case highlights the fact that the uniform civil code arena is likely to represent a process rather than an enactment, a continual negotiation more than a unilinear progression. Much of that process is likely to consist of the gradual accumulation of court decisions and particular pieces of legislation pointing in contradictory directions. In a careful review of cases litigated since the reform of the Hindu Code in the 1950s, Vasudha Dhagamwar, an activist legal scholar, traces a process of accumulation through the debates and litigation surrounding the Bombay Hindu Bigamous Marriages Act, the Hindu Marriage Act of 1955 (an element in the 'Hindu Code'), the Bombay Excommunications Act, the various versions of the Indian Adoption Bill, and the cases arising out of the Criminal Procedure Code of 1973 which led into the Shah Bano case. Dhagamwar believes that the process since independence has tended toward an erosion of the uniformity promoting tendencies.

Legal Pluralism as Multiculturalism; A Uniform Civil Code vs Minority Rights

When Rajiv Gandhi's Congress government in 1986 gave support to Muslim personal law by passing a Muslim Women [Protection of Rights] Act, his action raised a political storm. Sections of the Hindu nationalist Bharatiya Janta Party asserted that minorities were being pampered and privileged at the expense of the 'majority community', a euphemism for Hindus. The BJP's post-Shah Bano advocacy of a Uniform Civil Code had placed the contest between legal uniformity and legal pluralism at the centre of Indian political debate. It was a contest which fanned the flames of Hindu nationalism that leaped ever higher between 1985 and 1992. On December 6, 1992 thousands of Hindu nationalist youths wearing saffron headbands and wielding pick-axes destroyed the sixteenth century Babri Masjid (mosque built by the Mughal emperor Babur), while the Prime Minister of India stood helplessly by. They did so on the ground that it desecrated the site on which a temple to Lord Ram had stood. The internationally televised event became the symbol of a monumental crisis in India's self-definition as a secular state.

These events raise a number of questions. One is, how did Indian public discourse about difference move from the harmony of civilizations to the 'clash of civilizations'? Was the shift occasioned by the rise of Hindu nationalism, an aberration, or is it likely to endure?

As we write at the beginning of the 21st century, the flames of Hindu nationalism appear banked. In its quest to become the dominant party in a diverse multicultural land, the Hindu nationalist BJP has responded to the 1996 and 1999 elections by off-loading its communal, anti-minority planks. Advocacy of a Uniform Civil Code has been abandoned. The party has attempted to distance itself from extremist fringes. It has shown movement toward the policies that governments in a multi-cultural society find prudent to embrace, recognising and valuing difference rather than denigrating or eradicating it.

Representative of a new discourse that makes a Uniform Civil Code compatible with the continuing existence and integrity of personal law is S. P. Sathe's argument that 'the Constitution doubtless visualises the emergence of a uniform civil code, but does it mean a single law for all? . . . Within one nation there can exist a number of legal systems. In fact federal government,' he continues, 'means the coexistence of such multiple laws . . . . This means that Maharashtra may have its own family law different from that of Karnataka. In the U.S. each state has its own matrimonial law.'

A uniform law, Sathe argues, 'does not necessarily mean a common law but different personal laws based on uniform principles of equality of sexes and liberty for the individual . . . .'[13]

The struggle between legal uniformity and legal pluralism remains at the centre of public debate. We see the contestation as an open-ended story about balancing the uniformity of a civil code that protects minority rights.

Hopefully it will be the story of an unstable but viable equilibrium that combines the legal equality of human rights with a post-civilization 'multi-culturalism'. The language of multi-culturalism exhibits a family resemblance to the language of India's 18th century Orientalists, in their common belief that difference should be recognised and valued rather than denigrated or eradicated.

Conclusion

The idea of a uniform civil code carries no single meaning over historical time. Its advocates change, and change sides. Semioticists might call it a multi-valent signifier. We identity five possible meanings for the UCC.

One. The British implicitly moved toward a uniform civil code without calling it that. At the cultural level, making the law more uniform, standard-ising it, was an expression of rationalisation and modernisation. Uniformity of rules and regulations made it easier for those in charge of the 'steel frame' to administer justice, provide law and order and collect the revenue. Legal uniformity was in keeping with the formal organisations of the raj's admin-istrative state. It made the law more legible for bureaucrats who were strangers to India's diversity and villages. And it was believed to facilitate control. These rationales were equally congenial to those charged with ruling the post-colonial state.

Two. For modernist, rationalist nationalists a uniform civil code seemed to promise national integration. It would do for twentieth century India what nineteenth century nationalism was thought to have done for European states: dissolve or erase differences. It would help bring into being a nation whose people shared an identity congruent with state boundaries.

Three. For civil rights activists, those speaking for the marginalized and powerless, women, children, cultural and ethnic minorities, lower classes, a UCC signified the expansion of rights to categories of persons oppressed by patriarchal, gerontocratic, collective and oligarchic forms of social domination and control.

Four. For religious minorities, the uniform civil code signified an effort to erase the personal law of diverse communities. It posed a threat to their cultural identity, even to their cultural survival.

Five. For Hindu nationalists, a UCC promises a legal means to eliminate cultural difference and the 'special privileges' accorded to 'pampered minorities.' It would also rectify what they perceive as an injustice, the reform in the 1950s of Hindu personal law (the 'Hindu Code Bills') without reforming the Muslim personal law, making it possible in principle (but rarely in practice) for Muslim men to have four wives and to divorce at will.

At independence, about 1947–1950, the first three meanings of the UCC were dominant. In the last decade, especially since the destruction of the Babri Masjid in December 1992, the last two meanings have come to the fore, seeing the UCC as a means to diminish if not eradicate cultural pluralism. The foreground of these two meanings has changed the politics surrounding the UCC by problematising prior alignments. In contemporary Indian politics, civil and human rights activists who favour legal uniformity are accustomed to opposing the anti-Muslim Hindutva politics of Hindu nationalist politicians. Yet they find themselves on the same side with respect to a UCC. They think of a UCC as protecting and promoting the fundamental rights found in the Indian constitution and human rights found in international law. Feminists who typically oppose Muslim patriarchal controls are obliged to recognise that wiping out a repressive Muslim personal law is also an act of identity destruction. How to be pro civil and human rights and pro-feminist without being anti-Muslim? Where to go?

We have suggested that a uniform civil code can be conceptualised as a process rather than as a specific outcome, a process in which legal uniformity and legal pluralism jockey for dominance, not for the whole field. The liberal and progressive dream that it is the fate of difference to fade and for humanity increasingly to repair to a common mould;[14] and the additional dream of rationalists that it is the fate particularly of religion to fade away in face of the triumph of modern science has receded in the last two decades, not only in India but the wider world. In India, the opposition between legal pluralism and legal uniformity is not likely to yield a smooth progressive historical narrative in which society moves inexorably from the first to the second. Whether regarded as benign or malign, identity formation, in the form of religiously based personal law, seems to be alive and well.

The debate about the uniform civil code versus personal law need not be a zero-sum conflict. 'To put the choice as one between the personal law system and a uniform civil code is to pose the issue too sharply,' John Mansfield argues. He holds that it may be sensible to make distinctions and to adopt a 'particularizing approach,' such as 'has been going on since 1772.' (In Baird, op. cit., p. 175–6.) He bases his prescription on the importance of preserving difference, preserving, that is, the identity of ethnic or religious groups within a territorial state even while moving toward greater uniformity of rights.

Notes

1 From *Proceedings of the Committee of Circuit at Kasimbazaar*, 15 August, 1772, quoted in Bharatiya Vidya Bhavan, *History and Culture of the Indian People*, vol. 8, p. 361. For a longer discussion of Warren Hastings' role in the initial defining of difference, see Lloyd I. Rudolph and Susanne Hoeber Rudolph, 'Occidentalism and Orientalism: Perspectives on Legal Pluralism', in Sally Humphreys, ed., *Cultures of Scholarship*, Michigan, University of Michigan Press, 1997, pp. 21–51.

2 Stanley Wolpert, *A New History of India*, New York, Oxford University Press, 1982, p. 242.

3 Reginald Coupland, *The Indian Problem: Report on the Constitutional Problem in India*, 3 vols. in 1. New York, Oxford University Press, 1994, vol. 1, p. 23.

4 Marion Fowler, *Below the Peacock Fan: First Ladies of the Raj*, Harmondsworth, Penguin Books, 1988, p. 150.

5 The classic text for 'reform' is the late Eric Stokes, *The English Utilitarians in India*, Oxford, Clarendon Press, 1959. Part 111, 'Law and Government' on Macaulay as Law Member, and The Penal Code are especially relevant.

6 Gordon Johnson, 'India and Henry Maine' in Mushirul Hasan and Narauani Gupta, eds., *India's Colonial Encounter: Essays in Memory of Eric Stokes*, Delhi, Manohar, 1993, p. 31.

7 Eugene Irshick, *Politics and Social Conflict in South India: the Non-Brahman Movement and Tamil Separatism*, New Delhi, Oxford University Press, 1969.

8 See Albert Hirschman, *Exit, Voice and Loyalty*, Cambridge, Harvard University Press, 1970, for more on these concepts and how they can be applied.

9 Granville Austin, *The Indian Constitution*, New York, Oxford University Press, 1966, see pp. 151–4.

10 Another voice in support of legal pluralism is regionally dominant linguistic groups ('sons of the soil') who have demanded to be privileged in employment as against immigrants from other regional linguistic areas. The most notorious example is that of the Shiv Sena in Maharashtra who began by attacking Tamils and of late have been attacking Muslims from Bengal and Bangladesh. We will not deal with this form of legal pluralism here.

11 For a detailed discussion of the constituent assembly debate, see Vasudha Dhagamwar, 'Women, Children and the Constitution' in Robert D. Baird, ed., *Religion and Law in Independent India*, New Delhi, Manohar, 1993, pp. 218–21.

12 See a more detailed discussion of the case in its larger context in the struggle over secularism in Rudolph and Rudolph, *In Pursuit of Lakshmi: the Political Economy of the Indian State*, Chicago, Chicago University Press, 1987, pp. 44–6.

13 See S. P. Sathe in *Economic and Political Weekly*, Sept. 2, 1995; Imtiaz Ahmad, *Economic and Political Weekly*, Nov. 11, 1995; Mushirul Hasan, *Economic and Political Weekly*, Nov. 25, 1995; Saabeeha Bano, *op. cit.* See also John C. Mansfield in Baird, ed., *op. cit.*, pp. 175–6.

14 See Martha Nussbaum, ed., 'Patriotism or Cosmopolitanism', *Boston Review* vol. XIX, no. 5, 1994. For an application of the debate to India, see Lloyd Rudolph's contribution, 'The Occidental Tagore'.

© The Political Quarterly Publishing Co. Ltd. 2000

Religion and Democracy in Israel

EMANUELE OTTOLENGHI

SECTION 1(A) of Israel's *Basic Law: Human Dignity and Liberty* (1992) states that the law's purpose is 'to protect human dignity and liberty, in order to establish in a Basic Law the values of the State of Israel as a Jewish and democratic state.' The legislation, approved in 1992 and amended in 1994, is part of an ongoing process of constitution building, which has accompanied the state of Israel since its birth. Section 1(A) perhaps embodies the contradictions and difficulties arising from the idea of a Jewish state, within the framework of western democratic systems of government. These contradictions lie in the contested meaning of two terms, Jewish and democratic, whose different interpretations can lead, in their application, to synthesis, conflict or cohabitation. This article tries to address the complex relation between democracy and religion in the state of Israel.

Religion as a Source of Potential Divisiveness on the Eve of Independence

Zionism is the movement that calls for Jewish national self-determination in the land of Israel, the Jews' ancestral home. However, unlike forms of nationalism, Zionism has a problematic dimension that is rooted in Jewish tradition. Traditionally, Judaism viewed exile and dispersion as a divine punishment. Hence, exile was viewed as the normal condition of Jewish life, whose end would come through divine intervention at the end of days. While Jews could contribute to the end of exile through prayer and good deeds, the notion that human action could bring the Jewish people back to the land, as a reconstituted independent commonwealth, was blasphemous. By contrast to traditional religious views, Zionism considered exile as an anomaly and proposed to solve it by bringing the exiled people back to Israel, where it could create a modern state. Hence, it is no surprise that Zionism came from secular quarters, as a response to a loss of Jewish identity in 19th Century Europe, which followed emancipation and secularisation among Jews.

This loss of identity invited many answers: one was assimilation, the other Jewish nationalism. However, while Zionism was in principle a secular movement for national self-determination, it was rooted in religious tradition. While Zionist thinkers envisioned a secular, modern nation-state, national identity was based on a bond among dispersed people founded on religious tradition. Thus, though secularly oriented, Zionism used tradition as a source of legitimacy for its national claims, and could not disentangle

© The Political Quarterly Publishing Co. Ltd. 2000
Published by Blackwell Publishers, 108 Cowley Road, Oxford OX4 1JF, UK and 350 Main Street, Malden, MA 02148, USA

its argument for Jewish self-determination from religious identity.[1] This apparent contradiction meant that most secular Zionists could not do away with religion and actually needed it, lest the very justification for their movement's existence be weakened. However, Jewish tradition offered very little from the point of view of state building. Jewish law developed for nearly two thousand years without any consideration for the needs of reconciling religious rules with the practical needs of political sovereignty. Jews living in the Diaspora lacked political independence. Thus, political authority was in the hands of local rulers, who were in charge of all state powers. Because of this situation, Jewish law never had to reconcile religious observance of the Shabbat and of religious holidays, and the provision of basic public services. Hence, on the eve of independence, Jewish scholars were ill-equipped to provide answers to such questions as the running of hospital services, law enforcement, security, emergency, public transportation, and the provision of other public services, which a state must ensure 365 days a year. These activities, if performed on sacred days, involve a violation of religious rules. Yet they cannot be halted in a state. Jewish law simply could not provide an answer to this and many other similar dilemmas.

Traditionally, the religious answer to the inconsistency had always been that divine intervention at the end of days would resolve possible difficulties. Thus, on the eve of Israel's independence, the world of Jewish scholarship had not even started to address the question of how to reconcile Jewish law with the needs of a modern state. Nor had it completely accepted the very idea of Jewish political independence brought about by human agency.

Lacking a central religious authority entitled to give final binding answers on religious matters, Judaism is characterised by a high degree of pluralism and is open to many different interpretations. Therefore, although a thorough search for answers to the pressing questions that a democratic state would pose to religion could be undertaken, no univocal solution might be reached. Therefore, Judaism, Zionism, and democracy can be equally compatible, partially compatible, or incompatible, depending on who is the interpreter of any of the three terms. Several religious figures, indeed, undertook to address the issue in the months preceding independence, but they all ultimately failed to rise to the occasion.

The nature of responses that Zioism solicited among the religious leadership shows how different answers can be given on any subject of political relevance within Judaism. From the religious standpoint, Zionism posed a theological problem. By replacing divine intervention with human agency, Zionism was upsetting the basic eschatological vision of Judaism and its goal of collective salvation. Therefore, Zionism solicited two responses among religious Jews. The first was of utter rejection and opposition to the founding of a secular, modern Jewish state. This position was adopted by ultra-orthodox Jews, many of whom in 1912 organised themselves as a political party, the *Agudath Israel*.[2] The second was an attempt to reconcile the two positions: the product was religious Zionism, united under the banner of two parties (*Mizrachi* and *Hapoel Hamizrachi*), that later merged to form the National Religious Party (*Mafdal*) in the fifties.

While religious opposition to the creation of a Jewish state meant that those who adhered to this position refused in principle to participate in the Zionist effort, religious Zionism meant a thorough re-elaboration of the eschatological vision of redemption in Jewish tradition. This new vision viewed the establishment of Jewish sovereignty on the land of Israel (or portions thereof) as the first step on the path to redemption, where the coming of the Messiah would be not the initiating event, but its culminating moment. The Zionist effort was therefore viewed as 'the dawn of redemption'. Thus, contrary to other Zionist movements who viewed the enterprise of state-building in purely secular terms, the religious Zionists set out to ensure that the state would uphold religious tradition as much as possible. For religious Zionists, the goal of Zionism should not only be 'the ingathering of the exiles', but also the return of the exiles to tradition, as a precondition for the coming of the Messiah. This meant that the future state should actively engage in the enforcement of religious tradition within a sovereign Jewish polity.

The religious Zionists joined the Zionist movement already in the pre-state days, and this participation in the struggle for independence suggested that a conflict on the nature of the state would be forthcoming, unless their positions were accommodated by more secular views. In turn, the secular ambiguity *vis-à-vis* religion suggested that a compromise in defining the nature of the state was indeed possible, since for secular Zionists religion could not be entirely dispensed with.[3]

In addition, history's contingencies made the anti-Zionist religious position softer on the issue of a Jewish state and brought the ultra-orthodox as well into more active participation in the Zionist fabric of the state. In the aftermath of the Holocaust, and with the growing conflict in mandatory Palestine between Jews and Arabs, it was imperative for the Zionist leadership to ensure unity of the Jewish people in their support for a Jewish state. Ultra-orthodox parties on the other hand saw a Jewish state in a less negative light, as a chance for refuge to their flocks, which the Holocaust had almost entirely destroyed in Eastern Europe. Especially in light of the tragic events of the Holocaust, which had almost annihilated European Jewry, the creation of a Jewish state, albeit in contrast to traditional religious views, was seen nevertheless as a divine sign, which should not be opposed. In this context, the *Agudath Israel* sought reassurances from the secular Zionist leadership in June of 1947 that the soon-to-be established state would guarantee some basic religious demands. In exchange for these reassurances, the ultra-orthodox promised not to oppose the creation of a Jewish state. For the sake of unity, these guarantees were met in a letter, which was later to be referred to as the foundation of Israel's religious *status quo*.[4]

The *status quo* basically refers to the arrangements regarding religion, which were in place on the eve of independence. More specifically, the religious were concerned with four main issues:

— Jurisdictions over matters of marriage and divorce would stay with the religious courts;
— Religious education through their independent school systems would not be affected by the establishment of the state and would continue to function as previously;
— Religious holidays would be respected and adopted by the state as national holidays;
— Jewish dietary laws would be enforced in all public government catering.

While these promises were in no way legally binding, since they were given by the Executive of the Jewish Agency, and not by the government of a sovereign state, these arrangements had a degree of influence in determining the outcome of the constitutional debate, and have ultimately constituted one of the main sources of conflict between religious and secular during the entire history of the state of Israel.

State Building without a Constitution

Israel's Declaration of Independence makes explicit reference to the UN resolution on the partition of Palestine, which required the newly established states to call elections for a constitutional assembly, with the task of elaborating a democratic constitution. However, several factors hindered any attempt to give a constitution to the state of Israel. Born in the midst of a war of survival, the new state could not address the constitutional issue until February 1949, almost a year after independence. Instead, the provisional government had to effectively conduct a war, and ensure maximum unity and cohesion on the home front, despite the difficult divisions that characterised the *Yishuv*. One source of potential internal conflict was precisely the role of Jewish religious tradition in the new state.

Thus, the State had immediately to guarantee that several demands of the religious parties were met: dietary laws to be respected in the army, and subsequently in all public institutions. In addition, religious holidays became immediately national days of rest. The religious court structure left in place by the Ottoman and British mandatory rule was also kept, thus ensuring that religious courts would retain jurisdiction on personal matters such as marriage and divorce. The rabbinate was also entrusted with several vital public functions, including supervision of dietary laws' implementation in public places. All these developments took place in the first few months of independence, as the war was raging. In addition, the provisional authorities adopted several measures (later confirmed by the newly elected parliament) that established all key state institutions and ensured a smooth transition by retaining the entire body of mandatory laws. When the constitutional assembly gathered in February 1949 there was thus very little left to do in terms of institution building, other than formalising with legislation what had already been established in practice or through various ordinances by the provisional authorities. This situation had an importance consequence: there was no immediate and urgent need to write a constitution, since the basic framework of the state already existed, with institutions and services all in place and running. Besides, the arrangements that stemmed from the need to accommodate religious demands would pose several impracticalities to the elaboration of a western-styled written constitution. Many of the arrangements between the religious and the secular would probably fail to pass muster under an entrenched bill of rights that courts could enforce with the power of judicial review, unless the *status quo* could be entrenched as part of a constitution and thus protected from possible judicial intrusion.

However, there was an additional reason that worked against a constitution. The approval of a bill of rights, of checks and balances and other typical elements of a western-style limited government, could become a hindrance to the government's capability to effectively handle security threats and the permanent state of emergency in which the new state found itself. One could argue that both obstacles, religion and security, could still be handled within the framework of a constitution. But the dominant political culture of the day prevented any serious debate from taking place.[5] In particular, after initial preparations for a draft constitution, Prime Minister David Ben-Gurion made it clear that he opposed a constitution. The reasons for this position, beyond the rhetorical arguments that were put forward during the constitutional debate of 1949–1950, were that Ben-Gurion and his party, the *Mapai*, referred to rule without a constitution. A constitution would have established checks and balances, posing limits on government's powers, something that Ben-Gurion preferred to avoid.[6] As Eliezer Don-Yehiya has argued,

The centrality of the state . . . was thus strongly related to the cherished ideal of national unity and the process of 'nation-building.' The vital role of the state in this process was due to its being the only truly unifying factor for the Jewish people in both the political and the symbolic level. Only the state had the power and authority to overcome internal rivalries and conflicts of interests. Only the state could provide the various segments of the Jewish population with shared symbols of national identity and solidarity.[7]

Lack of a strong liberal culture among the founders hence played a part in the ultimate failure to adopt a constitution. In view of the fact that the strongest party and its leader did not see a constitution as vital, the religious parties went along, since they feared that a constitution could have endangered the role they wanted the new state to give to religion.

In addition, both religious and secular preferred a flexible arrangement on religious matters, since they saw the *status quo* as temporary, and both hoped that future changes in the demographic balance of the country would play to their advantage in altering the agreement. Thus, instead of searching a constitutional settlement on religious issues, the religious parties and *Mapai* coalesced to torpedo any attempt to adopt a constitution. But the convergence of religious and *Mapai*'s interests was only temporary, and it acted as the harbinger of later conflicts. The situation created by the constitution debate left the question of religion and state substantially open, and exposed the role of religion within the public sphere to continued conflict and readjustment during the intervening years. However, the bone of contention and the intensity of this conflict changed over time. The next section will sketch the two main issues that touch upon the relation between religion and democracy in Israel. The two issues are the definition of who is a Jew, and the solution to the Palestinian-Israeli conflict over the territories in the West Bank and Gaza. Thus, the first issue relates to the identity of the Jewish people as members of the state of Israel (either in fact or potentially, by right of return). The second issue relates to the identity of the Jewish state and the nature of its political regime, *vis-à-vis* its subjects.

Identity: Who is a Jew?

One of the main difficulties in the framing of a Jewish democracy has been the search for a legal definition of who is a Jew. Though Israel has professed itself a democracy since its Declaration of Independence was issued in 1948, Israel defines itself also as a Jewish state. As a fulfilment of one of the central goals of Zionism, the *Knesset* passed in 1950 the Law of Return, (4.L.S.I.114) which grants citizenship automatically to any Jewish individual who wishes to come to live in Israel. According to Ben-Gurion, the right of Jews to return to the land was an inherent component of being Jewish, the very essence of Jewishness. Accordingly, the state should facilitate the return of Jews by giving legal recognition to this right.

The combination of a modern legal concept such as citizenship and the ancient idea of membership in a nation through adherence to religion poses serious problems to the democratic implementation of membership in the political community. In Judaism, membership is acquired with kinship, by birth from a Jewish mother or religious conversion. In a democracy, membership is based on consent (active adherence to a political community through immigration and naturalisation for example), birth within the geographic boundaries of the state (*ius soli*), or descent (*ius sanguini*). However, descent is the most tenuous of the three criteria, since a claim to citizenship in a country loses strength in each generation, if descendants of a citizen dwell in foreign countries. By contrast, the *ius soli* is usually the strongest claim. Even when the *ius soli* is combined to the *ius sanguini*, the understanding of the concept of nationality is usually devoid of any religious content.

By contrast, Israel established a strong connection between a legal definition of citizenship to a religious understanding of nationhood.[8] The result has been that the Jewish identity of the state, its democratic nature, and the religious understanding of belonging to the Jewish people have been inextricably linked in a continuous struggle. By recognising to every Jew the right to acquire Israeli citizenship, the Law of Return has triggered a process whereby a set of legal rights and duties are granted to individuals on account of a criterion, membership in the Jewish nation, on which religious law traditionally held a monopoly. Hence, a religious basis for nationality has determined a situation where it is both impossible to disentangle religion from politics, or to ground citizenship on purely secular criteria, with the consequent danger of discrimination.

The secular nature of the state on the other hand prevented the adoption of strictly religious criteria in the bestowal of citizenship.[9] The wording of the Law of Return is such that many individuals who are not Jews from a strictly religious point of view can still enjoy a right of return as Jews. But the existence of religious courts, and their virtual monopoly on personal matters, suggests that individuals considered as Jews by the state might not necessarily be so in a religious court.

The potential for conflict did not take long to erupt. Since the late fifties the question 'Who is a Jew?' has periodically resurfaced in the national debate, often virulently. Though under the banner of different items, the question has focused on: religious versus secular understanding; individual versus collective understanding; conversions; dietary laws and public entertainment; Israel versus the Diaspora.

The 1988 electoral campaign was plagued by the bitter conflict over the question 'Who is a Jew?'. In response to the attempts of several religious parties to amend the Law of Return so as to require the state to use religious law as the *only* criterion for granting citizenship to Jews, Diaspora communities took an active role in the campaign and later on during the stages of coalition negotiations in order to prevent any such change from materializing.

The Supreme court had to address the request of a Polish monk Oswald Rufeisen, to be granted citizenship on the ground that he was Jewish by nationality, although Catholic by religion. The Court ruled that the criterion for deciding Rufeisen's case should be the understanding of the word by the average man on the street, and concluded that a convert to another religion could not, on this account, be considered a Jew. In the decision, the Court made it clear that religion and nationality could not be disentangled. At the same time, by using a criterion based on public perceptions, the Court disregarded religious law as a binding source for the case. Ironically, had the Court done so, Rufeisen, a Catholic monk, would have been entitled to recognition as a Jew on the basis of the Law of Return (something that the religious Minister of Interior was not prepared to do).

In *Shalit*,[10] the Court faced a similar case, where an army officer married to a non-Jewish woman requested that his children be registered as Jews, only on account of nationality, not religion. This time, though the request of Shalit was almost identical to the one put forward by Rufeisen, the Court went in the opposite direction and ruled in favour of Shalit. Though the reasoning was strictly based on administrative procedures and carefully avoided touching upon substantive questions, the logic behind was similar to Rufeisen, since it was a general understanding based on public perception that overcame religious criteria this time. Whereas in the first case the petitioner was Jewish according to religious law, but not Jewish according to public perception, in the second case the petitioners were not Jewish according to religious law, but perceived as such within society. The decision in *Shalit* prompted an amendment in the Law of Return that effectively reversed *Shalit* for future cases.

In *Miller*,[11] the Court dealt with the issue of conversions performed by non-orthodox authorities and accepted a claim by a convert that the state should recognise conversions performed abroad without questioning the religious authority of the rabbis involved. This decision carefully avoided once more addressing directly the question of 'Who is a Jew?' although it created a precedent for more recent clashes in the nineties, when non-orthodox movements have tried to press for a recognition of their religious authority *within* the state as well.

In *Raskin*,[12] the Court had to deal with a complaint filed by a Jerusalem's belly dancer. The case involved an alleged loss of contracts by the petitioner. Loss of contracts was apparently not due to her lack of skills, but to the fact that her habitual employers (hotels and restaurants) had been threatened by religious authorities to lose the *kashrut* certificate,[13] had they continued to provide their customers with 'immodest shows' in the environment where the food was served. In discussing the issue, the Court once again had to strike a balance between the claims of religious people and the claims of a secular view of society. Religious authorities in this case wanted to make sure that certain shows are not performed, and used the instrument of *kashrut* certificates to obtain this. The worker on the other hand tried to preserve a source of living through performances which, while they may offend certain religious views, nowadays are perfectly acceptable to the wider public. In deciding in favour of the belly dancer, the Court made it clear that the *kashrut* certificates were issued by religious authorities in pursuance of a *secular law* and therefore were not subject to a religious reading of the law. *Kashrut* was confined to food and the facilities where the food is prepared, nothing less but nothing more.

These examples illustrate the problematic role of religion in Israel, in the sphere of relations among Jews. The next section shall address the role played by religion in determining the identity of the Jewish State as a democracy *vis-à-vis* the Palestinians.

Land: Conquered or Freed?

An additional component of the difficult relation between religion and democracy was produced as a result of the victorious 1967 Six-Day War, when Israel conquered the West Bank and other territories from the adjacent Arab countries. The events surrounding the war had all the ingredients to suggest a reading in tune with the religious vision of the 'dawn of redemption.' There are two reasons for this statement. First of all, the events suggested at the time that the Jewish people had just narrowly escaped disaster and destruction at the hands of their neighbours, and turned an almost apocalyptic annihilation into a triumphant victory. The sweeping nature of the victory reinforced this feeling of trial and oppression turned into sudden triumph and fitted the main pattern of biblical tales of redemption. The second reason, though, is more important in the long term: most of the places that are holy to Judaism are located in the West Bank, which is also the heartland of the biblical Land of Israel. If the establishment of the state in 1948 had been read as the 'dawn of redemption', the conquest of what was viewed by many as Jewish land was interpreted as a further sign of a divine plan leading the Jewish people to the final redemption.

For many members of the religious public, the conquering of those lands was therefore part of the divine plan, and relinquishing the land was not a political option. Though once again, Judaism provides enough interpreting latitude to reach the opposite conclusion and therefore legitimise a territorial compromise even in the heartland of biblical Israel, the view that those territories should become an integral part of Israel prevailed within the religious camp.

Retaining the territories poses problematic questions on several standpoints. For the purpose of this chapter, though, a religious justification for the conquest, control and settlement of the West Bank puts Judaism on a collision course with democracy. The argument is well-known. The West Bank, with a population of over a million Palestinians, cannot be annexed without either putting an end to Israel as a democracy or as a Jewish state. If Palestinians were granted full citizenship, within a few years the state would have an Arab majority and would cease to be Jewish in its traits, character, ethos and legislation. If, on the other hand, Palestinians were denied citizenship and civil rights in order to preserve the Jewish character of the state, Israel would find itself in the uncomfortable situation of being a democracy only for Jews, and an *apartheid* regime for the rest of its inhabitants.

The territorial controversy has thus impinged on the difficult relation between Judaism and democracy, since an expansionist approach to it necessarily entails sacrificing one of the two principles for the sake of the other. This difficulty brings the debate back to the question of identity and the meaning of a Jewish state. For, in order to be *both* Jewish *and* democratic, the state must inevitably retain an overwhelming majority of Jews as its population, something that calls both for a territorial compromise and an identity compromise. Failure to adopt both might indeed suggest that in a Jewish state democracy and religion are at odds. The ongoing peace process, and the constitutional revolution expanding the liberal element of democracy at the expense of its Jewish element, suggests that Israel's challenge in the last decade has still been a quest for a reconciliation of its two founding aspirations, to be both Jewish and democratic.

Conclusion

This chapter has discussed the difficult relation between religion and democracy in Israel. Though not exhaustive, this overview has tried, through an illustration of the continuous struggle fought between religious and secular in parliament, courts, and public opinion, to show the intractability of the problem of a proper role for Jewish religion in the public square of a democracy. While an increasing awareness of individual civil rights can be detected in Israeli society, something which can only strength the democratic character of the state, what this discussion shows is that secular, liberal-minded institutions and individuals are themselves sometimes at a loss, when they try to confront the question of Jewish identity from a legal standpoint. The main difficulty lies precisely in the conscious knowledge that legitimacy within a democratic polity stems primarily from consent, rather than descent, and yet with uneasiness about getting rid of descent as the central factor in determining membership within the polity. Jewish nationhood cannot be detached from its religious tradition, whose bonding nature had preserved the Jews as a nation through the ages. The creation of a Jewish national identity that is entirely devoid of a religious connection does not seem to be a solution. Hence, the challenge ahead lies in the difficult attempt to reconcile within the public square, rather than privatise the conflicting criteria of kinship and consent as a premise for full participation in the destiny of a nation.

Notes

1 Cf. Giora Goldberg, 'Religious Zionism and the framing of a Constitution for Israel', in *Israel Studies*, 3, 1: Spring 1998, pp. 211–229.
2 For a discussion of various Jewish responses to Zionism, see Aviezer Ravitzky, *Messianism Zionism*, and *Jewish Religious Radicalism*, Chicago, University of Chicago Press, 1996. See Chapter 2 in particular for hostile religious responses to Zionism.
3 This was certainly Ben-Gurion's position, who made frequent reference to religious symbols as instruments of national identity. Cf. Ilan Peleg, 'Israel's Constitutional Order and Kulturkampf: the Role of Ben-Gurion', in *Israel Studies*, 3, 1: Spring 1998, pp. 230–47.
4 Cf. Menachem Friedman, 'The Structural Foundation for Religio-Political Accommodation in Israel: Fallacy and Reality', in S. Ilan Troen & Noah Lucas, eds., *Israel: The First Decade*, Albany, SUNY, 1995, pp. 51–82.
5 Cf. Ehud Sprinzak, 'Elite Illegalism in Israel and the Question of Democracy', in Ehud Sprinzak & Larry Diamond, eds., *Israel and Democracy under Stress*: Boulder, Lynne Rienner Press, 1993, pp. 173–98. See also Emanuel Rackman, *Israel's Emerging Constitution*, New York, Columbia University Press, 1995.
6 P. Strum, 'The Road Not Taken: Constitutional Non-Decision Making in 1948–50 and its impact on Civil Liberties in the Israeli Political Culture', in S. Ilan Troen & N. Lucas, *op. cit.*, p. 87: 'Not adopting a constitution . . . was in keeping with the

policy that had illuminated decision-making in the yishuv, which was to avoid all potentially disruptive decisions that were not absolutely necessary'.

7 Don-Yehiya, 'Political Religion in a New State: Ben Gurion's Mamlachtiyut', in S. Ilan Troen & N. Lucas, *op. cit.*, p. 176.

8 Cf. Benjamin Beit-Hallahmi, 'Back to the Fold: the Return to Judaism', in Zvi Sobel and Benjamin Beit-Hallahmi, eds., *Tradition, Innovation, and Conflict*, Albany, SUNY, 1991, p. 153: 'Laws respecting the establishment of religion have been made in Israel, and in this it is like many European countries. What is unique in Israel is the officially sanctioned relationship between religion, nationality and political rights. Being Jewish in Israel accords certain privileges, defined by law, as Jews constitute not only a religious group, but a national group as well'.

9 As the 1970 Amendment to the Law of Return has effectively sanctioned. Cf. *Law of Return* 1970, Amendment no. 2, 24 L.S.I. 28.

10 *Shalit v. Minister of Interior* (1970), 23(2) P.D. 477.

11 *Miller v. Minister of Interior* (1988), 40(4) P.D. 377.

12 *Raskin v. Jerusalem Religious Council*, H.C. 465/89, 44(2) P.D. 673.

13 The term *kashrut* refers to the suitability of edible substances to the dictates of Jewish dietary laws. Religious customers are entitled to know that the food they are about to consume meets the criteria established by religion, and restaurants and hotels who want to be certified as kosher must exhibit a permit, issued by religious authorities, that their food and kitchen utensils meet the standards established by religious law. The permits are issued by a religious authority, in pursuance of a Knesset statute which regulates the issue.

14 Cf. Yeshayahu Leibowitz, 'Judaism, Human Values, and the Jewish State', in Eliezer Godlam, ed., Cambridge MA, Harvard University Press, 1992, pp. 226–7. 'Counterfeit religion identifies national interests with the service of God and imputes to the state which is only an instrument serving human needs supreme value from a religious standpoint. The 'halakhic' reasons for remaining in control of the territories are ridiculous, since the state of Israel does not acknowledge the authority of the Torah and the majority of its Jewish inhabitants reject the imperative demands of its Mitzvoth. The conquest of the land by the army of the state of Israel is a great and impressive national achievement for every nationally conscious Jew, whether religious or secular. However, the conquest itself has no religious significance. Not every 'return to Zion' is a religiously significant achievement: one sort of return which may be described in the words of the prophet: 'When you entered you defiled the land and made my heritage an abomination' (Jer. 2:7).'

Islam, Politics and Democracy: Mohamed Talbi and Islamic Modernism

RONALD L. NETTLER

Backgrounds, Contexts and Intellectual Definitions

Since the 1960s, much has been said and written on modern Islam and its relation to politics. Much of this has been on aspects of the 'Islamist' (political Islamic) movements and ideologies. This was perhaps a 'natural' response to what appeared an important (and for some a worrying) trend.[1] Until recently, relatively little attention had been given to the 'non-political' Muslim thinkers and intellectual trends, especially those who seek a particular sort of conceptual accommodation between modernity and tradition. Now more widely recognised and discussed, this 'modernist' thought has become more prominent. In its central preoccupation with Islam and modernity, it evinces certain basic features: an apolitical conception of Islam; a contextual/critical/historical exegesis of the Qur'an and *hadith* literature; a 'liberal' political and social Islamic ethos of human rights, pluralism and democracy; a religious individualism; and a rejection of the presumed authoritative status of the traditional schools of Islamic law and theology. Other features might be added to these, and certainly some writers would emphasise some (or one) more than others. But as a *complex of ideas* these are to be found through a certain range of thinkers over a period of time, beginning in the late 19th century until the end of the 20th. The earlier periods saw a rather 'muted' modernism in contrast to recent years, with modernist features subtly present in a variety of intellectual schools; but, then, other outlooks were earlier also 'muted', more diffuse and less discernible as discrete lines of thought. Islamic thought in the 20th century was still taking shape. Thus Modernism has appeared in a more pronounced way in the writings of certain Muslim intellectuals from the 1960s onwards, with the crystallisation of all the major intellectual lines. It has been present in various geographical areas including North Africa, the Arab Middle East, Iran, Turkey, South and Southeast Asia, South Africa, Western Europe and North America. Though smaller in numbers and, most likely, far less broadly influential than Islamist intellectuals in the same period, the modernists represent a highly particular intellectual reconsideration of traditional thought with the construction of a 'new Islam'. To their minds, this 'new Islam' is not only consonant with the modern world, but embodies the original essence or core of the tradition. It is 'new' only in being a 'rediscovery' of the 'original' Islam of the early period.

Published by Blackwell Publishers, 108 Cowley Road, Oxford OX4 1JF, UK and 350 Main Street, Malden, MA 02148, USA

(This emphasis on seeking Islam's true nature *mainly* in its earliest period in the Medina of Muhammad, thereby effacing [or at least marginalising] the whole of its subsequent development, is pronounced in much of modern Islamic thought. It is qualitatively and quantitatively a departure from the pre-modern mainstream Islamic thought). Mohamed Talbi shall serve here as an example of this type of modernist thinker and intellectual trend.

Mohamed Talbi

Professor Mohamed Talbi is a leading contemporary modernist Muslim thinker. Born in Tunis in 1921[2] and educated there and later in Paris, Talbi has had an illustrious career, both as a historian of medieval North Africa and (our focus here) as a major theoretical thinker on Islam's nature and mission in the modern world. Among Talbi's modern interests have been religion and politics, Islam and democracy, Islam and human rights, women in Islam and Islam and religious pluralism, in the wider context of his general thinking on Qur'anic exegesis, historical analysis and religious epistemology. In his discussions of these subjects, Talbi makes clear his dependence on the Qur'an and other traditional religious sources, while evincing also an easy incorporation of certain modern Western Ideas. Indeed, Talbi's own description of his upbringing and education in Tunisia, and in particular his doctoral studies in post-War Paris, reflects a relaxed attitude towards synthesising Islamic and modern Western thought, in both of which he possesses the requisite learning to effect such an integration. Thus, for example, with no hint of intellectual defensiveness or Islamic apologetics, Talbi recounts his educational experience in Paris, with particular reference to the debt he feels towards Western thinkers and teachers whose ideas and methods helped him to revise his own intellectual and religious thought: From the Existentialism of Sartre he learned 'an antidote with which to offset exaggerated Idealism'; from Marxism, despite his disagreement with it, he learned that 'economic forces were . . . among the basic agents influencing and determining history'; from Freud he learned about the 'unconscious motivations' which so often directed men and events. This was 'humbling', says Talbi, as it pointed up the limitations of human knowledge and understanding. And from his teachers at the Sorbonne—in particular the great orientalists Regis Blachère and Louis Massignon—Talbi learned about Islam in ways which gave him a valuable new perspective.

Imbued with this breadth of vision and a commitment to rediscovering the truth of Islam for reconstruction and renewal in the modern world, Talbi has been radical in his Islamic thought, in the basic sense of going to the roots of the tradition as he sought and found them. There he discovered an Islam which could be seen as being not just in tune with the best of modern values, but even as embodying and representing them in the deepest way. Despite his reiterated humble historian's disclaimer concerning knowledge of what Islam really is, Talbi found in the Qur'an and other early sources and historical documents evidence of Islamic mercy, critical reason, freedom and pluralism, to cite but some of his ideas about the nature of Islam.[3]

What is Islam?

This question—not pursued by reflective Muslims in such a direct and vigorous way since Islam's formative period, and then in quite a different fashion—has, implicitly or explicitly, motivated and engaged most of the important Muslim intellectuals working *within the tradition* (not the secularists) in the 20th century. Its centrality reflects the modern situation of Islamic eclipse at the hands of Western imperial presence, domination and influence, with the attendant erosion of Islamic institutional organisation and intellectual life. The framework of traditional institutions and the ideas developed from within it were now in most places more vestigial remains than living reality. In their stead were 'hybrid societies', formally in structure and appearance modern nation-states, but internally a swirling mix of 'the old' and 'the new'. The well-known tensions engendered by this conflict 'between tradition and modernity', as the stock cliché would have it, among other things undermined with doubt and uncertainty the foundations and legitimacy of received religious thought. This condition was particularly acute among the 'non-official' intellectuals who sought modern meaning in the received texts, especially the Qur'an; their challenge was greater than that of the 'official' institutional religious scholars and authorities, ('*ulama*') or the secular intellectuals. But it was this group who have been most cited and whose presence and contribution to modern Islamic intellectual life have been most prominent.[4] Very broadly, they encompass 'fundamentalists' (political 'Islamists'), 'modernists' and 'liberals'—and all others whose religious commitment remains firm but for whom the apparent dissonance between the official religious intellectual approach and the modern Islamic situation is too great to countenance.[5] For these thinkers, the question, 'What is Islam?' has been central-even when they have not explicitly asked it. Let us, however, briefly, survey these views, bearing in mind our own emphasis here on the modernist outlook.

For most Islamists, the answer has been that Islam is, first and foremost, a particular sort of polity and society, through which religion is most perfectly expressed in accord with the divine will. Individual piety and practice, enjoined by relevation as the path to individual salvation, are also integral to the collective end of state and society. Indeed, it is all of one fabric, which in its present tattered state may only begin to be repaired with the personal return to God of individual Muslims. For the Egyptian Sayyid Qutb, (1906–1966), perhaps the most important Islamist thinker of the 20th century, there are two intertwined dimensions of Islam: personal observance and a proper Islamic political and social order. Qutb, like most Islamists, thought that though personal return is basic and essential, it is ultimately absorbed in the more general political and social dimension of Islam. It is through the Islamic

© The Political Quarterly Publishing Co. Ltd. 2000

political expression that the world will acknowledge Islam's truth and by which Islam will liberate humanity from the depravity of its secularism and the corruption of its religions.[6] All of this is in total contrast with the views of the modernists. Though their answers may define Islam in various terms, with different thinkers emphasising different features, the modernists usually downplay the political and social dimension, rigorously and in quite a thoroughgoing way. Islam as polity and society may even be effaced altogether as an essential feature of the tradition, being viewed as secular constructs having no Islamic religious meaning or content. The individual Muslim then becomes all-important as the locus of Islam and his personal relationship with God and Text form the basis of the tradition. There may be as many Islams here as there are Muslims.[7] Ethical principles and universalistic teachings are emphasised. The notion of authoritive persons and institutions becomes meaningless. The Qur'an and other source-texts are given historical-critical-contextual treatment, in contrast to Islamist exegesis, which tends towards a more literalistic method of interpretation. While both Islamists and modernists usually abjure the authoritative monolithic authority (*taqlid*) of the schools of Islamic law and theology, the Islamists seek a revision of this notion towards a new (their own) authoritative structure and the modernists reject any such formal collective authority, leaving it to the individual Muslim to make the ultimate decisions. Finally, modernists may be distinguished here not only from Islamists, but also from Islamic liberals who, while agreeing with the modernists on many points, like the Islamists cannot accept the modernists' rejection of a political nature for Islam. This may well be the main feature distinguishing the modernists from all others. As a modernist, Talbi evinces this idea and those others mentioned above in his own particular way and from his own perspective. I shall look especially at three aspects in Talbi's thought: his answer to the question, 'What is Islam?'; religion and politics; Islam and democracy. These subjects are obviously related to one another, and I shall organise my own discussion so as to point up the integration of the issues in Talbi's formulation.

Talbi's Answer

Talbi understands Islam as personal piety and worship of God in a framework of revealed universal ethical principles which are to be implemented in human life. The Qur'an in his view is not only central, but it constitutes virtually the whole of the tradition. 'The Qur'an *is* Islam'.[8] Though (in keeping with most traditional doctrine) Talbi sees the Qur'an as God's literal word, for him it contains both universal ethical principles and more detailed timebound injunctions meant by God only for the particular situations of their revelation. Thus in his view, the timeless 'wheat' of revelation must be separated from its timebound 'chaff'. If this is not done, the continuing attempts of religious authorities and others in each generation to understand and to apply the Qur'an to real life are inevitably reduced to applying the Book's timebound injunctions to situations for which they are inappropriate. For Talbi, this constitutes an unfortunate fossilisation of a dynamic living revelation, whose very genius lies in its continuing relevance and applicability to life in all times and places. Islam in its personal pietism and Qur'anic ethical universalism is meant to do this. However, says Talbi, for much of Islam's history after its early Prophetic period, its development was, more often than not, along the wrong path of misplaced rigid application of such inappropriate ancient teachings—on the mistaken assumption that this would be the implementation of God's will. To be sure, there were great figures and schools which may be invoked as models of a more authentic and 'progressive' Islamic thinking, but the larger picture for Talbi is that of a sadly misplaced 'conservatism'. This 'conservatism' is as much a feature of modern and contemporary Islamic thought, says Talbi, as of the classical and medieval schools. Indeed, Talbi claims, to his amazement and consternation, with respect to at least one important issue–the status and treatment of women in Islam—certain medieval Qur'anic exegetes were more liberal and far-reaching in their approach than were some of the modern 'reformist' luminaries. Here the particular problem is a proper understanding of a certain verse in the text which would appear to sanction physical means to curb disobedient wives where other, milder, sanctions have failed. Talbi argues that the main exegetical and legal traditions have taken this literally and approved its application. For him, this interpretation and practice were wrong. In his reading, this verse must be seen in its historical context, which renders it obsolete in later periods, when true Islamic 'feminism' is to be applied.

Religion and Politics

In Talbi's view, a major accompaniment of this conservative development in Islamic religious thought and practice was the conception and attempted implementation of an Islamic political ideal. Conceived as a 'proper' Islamic government and polity, this political ideal, again, derived from the erroneous model of Islamic religion as an ongoing quest to implement what were in reality timebound customs, practices and Qur'anic injunctions. But for Talbi just as true religion is ethical, pietistic and apolitical, politics on its side should be divorced from any such detailed religious conceptions and injunctions—indeed, from any religion at all. From both sides, then, this mix of religion and politics was, in his view, ill-conceived and misbegotten. There is no Islamic governmental form, argues Talbi, and if there were he would not follow it anyway, as it would most likely turn out to be relevant only to a particular time and place. Indeed, says Talbi, 'the Qur'an is not a constitution', as some would claim, and if it were he would not adhere to that aspect of his faith, as, like most constitutions, its usefulness and validity would have been corroded in the passage of time. The political Islamists of our time (like their pre-modern predecessors) have taken the notion of a 'proper' Islamic form of government to extremes, thereby attempting to coerce fellow Muslims into rigid political arrangements towards compliance with some of tradition's now irrelevant and (sometimes) deleterious injunctions. This is necessarily tyrannical and harsh, impeding—even destroying—any movement towards freedom, human rights, pluralism and true democracy, some of the features which characterise Talbi's own conception of a proper politics for the Islamic world. This is a politics which is universal and not enjoined by Islam *as an Islamic political or governmental form*, but rather as Islam's universal human value which, in our historical epoch, would most likely be expressed in democracy. But in which ways—if any—are these features Islamic and which Islamic precedents—if any—may be invoked in their support? Talbi addresses these questions from different angles, and in particular in his response to a question concerning the popular modern liberal Islamic notion that the ancient Arabian (and Qur'anic) institution of *shura*, 'consultation' by rulers with their subjects, constitutes an early form of Islamic democracy which may therefore be considered as a sacred precedent justifying (even enjoining) democracy in the Islamic world today.

Islam and Democracy

Talbi rejects this direct association between *shura* and democracy. He argues that, while desirable in itself, *shura* is from a time and place which had no conception of democracy as we know it. Indeed, says Talbi, neither Islam nor Western civilisation had this democratic conception before the modern period, when democracy, as political idea and practice was born—at least not democracy in our modern meaning of the term. For Talbi, this democracy means the voice of the many ('the people') determining who rules and how they rule, with the associated notions of universal human rights, freedom of expression, religious pluralism and equality before the law. 'True democracy' of this kind (and not any of the repressive systems which call themselves 'democracy') is for Talbi the proper political form for our age, as it embodies those values which for him constitute part of the original true Islam. In some future age, he argues, other governmental forms may do the job better and supersede democracy. *Shura*, though, again, not really similar to this, does in its difference contain *some elements* of true democracy, in particular the concern for the subject and the subject's views, which is integral to the very idea of consultation. Individual freedom, *of sorts*, is also implied here, says Talbi. However, *shura is not an institution unique to early Islam in Arabia*: it existed in pre-Islamic Arabian tribal society and from there found its way into early Islam. *Shura*'s Islamic identity, then, remains true, but in a somewhat reduced and less unique way. Talbi, again, finds the other components of democracy in the Qur'an as basic Islamic (and universal) values. These divine ethical principles—deeply Islamic and universally human, and known through reason as well as revelation—may at most constitute a sort of 'bridge' between Islam and modern democracy. But democracy, it must again be emphasised, never did exist in the Islamic world. Modern democracy implemented in the Islamic world could, for Talbi, then be considered a fulfillment of God's will, without the (erroneous) claim that it had already existed in Arabia at the time of the Prophet as *shura* or as any other traditional value or practice; and without the notion that it is in any sense 'Islamic'. Again, for Talbi the 'political' and the 'religious' are for Islam separate conceptual categories and unrelated phenomena. Muslims who would now (wisely, in Talbi's view) institute democratic government in their societies, would do this, then, *as human beings* who wish to do what is right—not as Muslims instituting a religiously enjoined Islamic governmental form.

The Significance of Islamic Modernism

Mohamed Talbi's ideas on these (and related) subjects do *in broad compass* coincide with those of the other Muslim thinkers whom we refer to as modernists. The task of historical and intellectual analysis of these ideas and their status and significance in the contemporary Islamic world in great part still lies before us. This will require a serious grappling with some rather difficult writings in their original Arabic (and other) language. Central to this task will be the need to discern the intellectual contexts of and influences, pre-modern as well as modern, on the modernist thought and to delineate precisely the features common to the modernist thinkers. Designation of common features would then provide a foundation for more detailed iden- tification of the trend. This has in fact to some extent now been pursued, even if in a preliminary fashion. Apart from some earlier work, two recent books and one article have in particular figured prominently in discussion of this issue. The books,[9] collections of modernist writings and writings about modernists, assume the existence of such a trend in general descriptions and reinforce this judgment with specific texts and analyses. The article, by the American social anthropologist of Islam Dale F. Eickelman, is quite far- reaching in its assertions of an 'Islamic Reformation'[10] embodied in this modernism and having in Islam a role similar to that played by the earlier Protestant Reformation in Europe. Controversial and provocative in his argument, Eickelman has made explicit some of the underlying ideas in other discussions of Islamic modernism. Whether 'right' or 'wrong', his original thesis provides a useful focal point now for attempts at making some sense of the modernist phenomenon—sense which will ultimately be made fully only with more detailed assessments of individual modernist thinkers.[11] Eickelman's views may serve us here as a means of placing Mohamed Talbi more generally in the Islamic modernism of which he is so integral a part and of seeing that modernism itself in larger historical perspective.

'Inside the Islamic Reformation'

In his article thus titled, Eickelman, as social anthropologist, writes from the broad perspective of the mass media, particularly television and mass education, in the Muslim world in recent years. These elements, in a general context of continuing modernisation and Westernisation, have in Eickelman's view engendered an emerging individualism which has rendered both ordinary believers and independent religious thinkers more critical of the official interpretations in matters of belief and practice. Though for Eickelman this phenomenon does involve some religious 'fanaticism', that 'is far from the whole story'. For at the same time, particularly among certain of the independent thinkers, the 'new criticism' of tradition has as well given rise to the sort of modernism discussed above. Eickelman's main example here is Muhammad Shahrur, a contemporary Syrian civil engineer who writes on religious matters. Shahrur's book, *The Book and the Qur'an: A Contemporary Interpretation* (1990), 'has sold tens of thousands of copies', despite an official ban in many Middle Eastern countries. With a historical-critical approach to the text much like that of Talbi, Shahrur asks Muslims to interpret and redefine the Book's contents *for themselves and their own time and place*. He is also, like Talbi, strongly apolitical in his Islam, but tending towards democracy as his chosen political form. Eickelman mentions other thinkers in various Muslim countries who share these (and similar) views. All of this ferment, popular as well as elitist, engendered, as it has been in Eickelman's view, by the 'catalysts of change' of mass media and mass education, is an 'Islamic Reformation'. So significant is this that 'We will look back on the latter years of the 20th century as a time of change as profound for the Muslim world as the Protestant Reformation was for Christendom'. Though various (sometimes conflicting) trends make up this Islamic Reformation, it is clear that its leading edge and most significant aspect for Eickelman is the modernism of thinkers such as Shahrur and Talbi. With them lies the intellectual rationale for what Eickelman sees as the core feature of the Islamic Reformation and which he explains as sweeping changes whereby 'Islam has been democratised'. This means that, 'Like Martin Luther at the Diet of Worms in 1521, more and more Muslims today claim attachment to God's unmediated word, as interpreted only by their conscience'. Such free, individualistic interpretation of Islam would, then, in Eickelman's terms be both prerequisite for and the logical conclusion of Talbi's 'depoliticisation' of Islam. For the structural features (mass media and education) which Eickelman posits as lying beneath the Reformation would usually militate against *any prescribed form* of Islamic political order. The 'democratisation' of Islam as Eickelman sees it here would (has ?) for Talbi inexorably lead to an apolitical conception of a personal, pietistic Islam best developed in a (non-Islamic) democratic society. Here believer and Book would cultivate their private relationship in a personal, private manner—in the 'Protestant' fashion.

While Eickelman's thesis does cast some light on modernist figures such as Mohamed Talbi and on the 'new individualism', his comparison with the Protestant Reformation certainly does not give all the answers. Eickelman himself acknowledges, for example, that unlike Luther the present-day Islamic trends of apolitical individualism do not have a single authority against which they are rebelling. Also, promulgation of this thesis would require a developed body of theoretical thought dealing for modern Islam with the sorts of complex issues various scholars have discussed in their thinking on the situation of Protestantism in Europe. Eickelman's 'catalysts of change' in the media and education are, moreover, themselves products of the Islamic contacts and conflicts with the West in the modern period in which the features of Islamic traditional society have been either effaced or deeply changed, within a very short period. He says little about this. Yet, in my view, Eickelman's approach may serve as a rudimentary framework of issues and questions which could be useful in assessing not only the ideas of modernists such as Talbi, but the situation in which Islamic modernism arose. Individual thinkers would then need to be analysed rigorously in the way called for above, while at the same time these larger contextual issues would require a similarly rigorous treatment. In any case, insofar as Mohamed Talbi and his modernist colleagues constitute a serious break with most of mainstream traditional Islam (and they do), Eickelman's thesis provides an interesting *provisional* notion of meaning and context. Talbi and Eickelman (and many others) if properly understood have in their own ways put paid to the common notion of a monolithic 'political Islam' as Islam's main expression in our time.

Notes

1 The Islamists and their sometimes disruptive activities brought Islam to the attention of the West. With key events such as the revolution in Iran, a media-driven conception of Islam as mainly a militant 'political religion' took hold among a general Western population who had had little occasion to think about this neighbouring civilisation. Scholars too, chose to focus on political Islam, producing often important work, but in the process neglecting other aspects.

2 Talbi provides a good autobiographical sketch in a book of questions posed to him with his answers, titled ʿIyal Allah; Afkar Jadida fi ʿAlaqat al-Muslim bi Nafsihi wa bi al-Akhirin: Families of God: New Ideas Concerning the Relation of the Muslim to Himself and Others. Tunis, Ceres Editions, 1992. See pages 21–45. This book is the basic source from which I shall draw in references to Talbi's ideas; another source is Talbi's work titled Umma al-Wasat: al-Islam wa Tahadiyyat al-Muʿasara: The Community of Moderation: Islam and the Challenges of Modernity. Tunis, Ceres Editions, 1996. Some of my own writings deal in detail with the aspect of Talbi's thought discussed in the present chapter; in particular see: "Mohamed Talbi: 'For Dialogue Between all Religions'", in Ronald L. Nettler and Suha Taji-Farouki, Muslim–Jewish Encounters: Intellectual Traditions and Modern Politics. Reading, Harwood, 1998, pp. 171–201; and 'Mohamed Talbi's Ideas on Islam and Politics:

A Conception of Islam for the Modern World' in John Cooper, Ronald Nettler and Mohamed Mahmoud, eds., *Islam and Modernity: Muslim Intellectuals Respond.* London, I. B. Tauris, 1998, pp. 129–56.

3 One of Talbi's most comprehensive modernist notions of Islam is that it is '. . . *reconciliation and peace* in its essence and in its mission', (italics mine).

4 The 'official thinkers', the *'ulama'*, have by and large remained well within the pre-modern textual traditions, though in recent years many have evinced new Islamic concerns going beyond those texts.

5 This typology here and in its further elaboration in this chapter is admittedly somewhat arbitrary, but I hope it does also describe a reality.

6 See: Ronald L. Nettler, 'Guidelines for the Islamic Community: Sayyid Qutb's political Interpretation of the Qur'an', in *Journal of Political Ideologies,* 1996, pp. 183–86.

7 The implications here for the central traditional Islamic notion of the *Umma Muslima,* the Muslim Community, are indeed profound.

8 In a public lecture in Oxford in October, 1999, Talbi made this statement, which he explained as meaning that a Muslim needs almost nothing else for the proper observance of the faith.

9 Charles Kurzman, ed., *Liberal Islam: A Sourcebook.* New York, Oxford University Press, 1998; John Cooper, Ronald Nettler and Mohamed Mahmoud, eds., *Islam and Modernity: Muslim Intellectuals Respond.* London, I. B. Tauris, 1998.

10 Dale F. Eickelman, 'Inside the Islamic Reformation', *The Wilson Quarterly.* Winter, 1998, pp. 80–9.

11 This movement between detailed studies of individual thinkers and a continuous refining of the conception of the trend in which they operate will be the necessary process of clarification.

Trajectories of Political Islam:
Egypt, Iran and Turkey

SAMI ZUBAIDA

AT the time of the Iranian Revolution in 1978–9, Islam, or what was called 'Islamic Fundamentalism' seemed to be on the ascendance on the world stage. Coupled with the loss of credibility of leftist and nationalist ideologies and movements in the region, Islam seemed to present an alternative idiom and impetus of opposition and the construction of alternatives. Islamic movements came to the fore in many countries. The political arenas were dominated by the Islamic tide. Islam became the feared medium of subversion and revolt for many governments and for the world powers intent on maintaining hegemony. Leaders rushed to adopt Islamic positions to compete with the opposition. This was the 'charismatic' period of political and revolutionary Islam. Indeed, in Iran and in Egypt there were distinct messianic elements in the Islamic movements, as we shall see.

Charisma, however, is by its very nature transitional. In Max Weber's terms, sooner or later it is 'routinised'[1]. Weber's postulated dynamic between charisma and its routinisation is an apt metaphor for the transformations of political Islam in the last few decades. Khomeini was the prototype of a charismatic leader, predominantly for Iran, but through world media for the whole of the Muslim world (much like Mao, Castro or Guevara played that role for the international left at a previous moment). His personal authority and novel political interpretation of Shi'i doctrine appeared to form the bases of the Revolution and subsequent Republic. Above all, he challenged the Americans and the West in the name of Islamic authenticity and emerged victorious (or so it seemed). Among the Iranian masses, Khomeini's title of 'Imam' was stretched to a connotation of 'Imamul-Zaman', the awaited Messiah. Throughout the Middle East the Iranian Revolution and its leader became a shining example and an inspiration (despite Sunni misgivings about its Shi'i character). It proved that 'authentic' Islam is a revolutionary ideology which could inspire the masses because it spoke to them in their own language (unlike 'imported' Western ideas of the left and the nationalists).

While Egypt lacked a Khomeini figure, it featured charismatic ideas which spawned charismatic communities.[2] Such were Sayyed Qutb's ideas: a society is only Muslim if it lives in accordance with God's law (*hakimiyyat allah*) as revealed in His Book. All supposedly Muslim countries are governed with man-made law, and as such they are not Muslim, but in a state of *jahiliyya*, ignorance, with connotations of barbarism, a term commonly used to designate pre-Islamic society[3]. In this situation a true Muslim can only follow the example of the 'first generation' of Muslims, of the Prophet and

Published by Blackwell Publishers, 108 Cowley Road, Oxford OX4 1JF, UK and 350 Main Street, Malden, MA 02148, USA

his small band of followers, who lived by the Book, and struggled to convert the *jahili* world to their faith. Now, too, a vanguard (*tali'a*) of Muslims must follow in their footsteps, insulate themselves from the sins of *jahili* society, fortify themselves with faith, numbers (converts) and arms, to eventually convert the world to God's rule. These ideas are charismatic in that they introduce a radical break with the world as it is in the name of sacred doctrine, much like Weber's Old Testament prophets who proclaimed 'It is written . . . but I say unto you . . .'. Qutb was no charismatic leader, and in any case spent his last years in prison before his execution in 1965. It was in the 1970s that his ideas constituted the bases for the formation of radical groups, notably Jihad and Jama'at al-Muslimun (so-called Takfir wal-Hijra group). These, especially the latter, constituted themselves as vanguard communities, insulated from *jahili* society, whom they considered as non-Muslim, and whose lives and property (and women) were forfeit to true Muslims. In the sense of this break from normal society and Messianic vision of a sacred realm which they were to create, we may see them as 'charismatic' communities.

We may think of 1970–1982 as the charismatic period of political Islam. Articulated on to this charisma were strands of leftist revolutionary ideas. Ali Shari'ati (d. 1977) in Iran preached revolutionary ('red') Shi'ism, which seemed to consist of Marxist and Fanonist themes, read by Shari'ati into the Quran and Shi'i doctrine[4]. His ideas were enormously attractive to a generation of intellectuals and activists seeking revolution and liberation, but with an 'authentic' cultural lineage. These strands of leftist Islam played a crucial role in the 1979 Revolution, and in the 'socialist' and populist stances of the early revolutionary years. In Egypt, too, many of the leftists and Nasserists turned to Islam as the authentic vehicle of popular contestation and national liberation. Prominent figure of the Egyptian left, such as Hassan Hanafi, Tariq al-Bishri and Adel Hussain, led this trend, the first issuing a review with the title, *Al-Yasar al-Islami*, the Islamic left. These were and remain influential figures in public life, but with nothing like the charismatic appeal of Shari'ati at an earlier point. Nevertheless, it was these figures, and their equivalents in Lebanon and Iraq, who gave a distinctly *political* stamp to the Islamic revival, and it was the demise of this current in favour of conservative moralism which Olivier Roy described in his book *The Failure of Political Islam*[5].

The 'failure' of political Islam is part of the process of the routinisation of charisma. The fervour and the expectation of almost supernatural transformations (characteristic of Messianism) which stamped the charismatic period wanted in Iran, Egypt and throughout the region. The establishment of the Islamic Republic and the emergence of the conservative mollas as its masters directed government and society towards a legalistic and disciplinary ethos, a process of 'rationalisation'. The revolutionaries and liberationists were either violently suppressed or co-opted. The Islamic left suffered repeated defeats for its 'socialist' policies (labour laws, nationalisation, land reform, welfare) to the conservatives who interpreted sacred law as favouring absolute property rights[6]. The ruling mollas and their clients prospered (often through control of state and foundation resources), while the economy floundered and large sectors of the salariate impoverished (including the middle class intelligentsia). In Egypt the radical Qutbist groups became ever more isolated, and in any case settled to enforce communal morality and discipline in their fiefs while fighting the government. The main initiative in Islamic advocacy passed to the conservatives, many of them part of state institutions. The Islamic left and liberals are seeking to integrate into a legal opposition as part of a regular political process, but facing resistance and persecution from the authorities with the acquiescence if not the support of Islamic conservatives.

The question is now being asked whether the Islamic current has 'peaked' and is now on the decline? This is too simplistic a generalisation. The answer I give here is in terms of the 'routinisation' of charisma, and, in the case of Iran, one of rationalisation of government and the economy. Islamic movements, with their many trends and currents, political and social, have become integrated into the politics and society of their respective countries. They have acquired particular characters and directions moulded by the socio-political cultures and historical conjunctures of their respective societies. Before proceeding to examine these developments in the three countries, let me present a typology of ideological and social directions of Islamic movements, one that emerges from the work of many commentators, including Ayubi, Roy, as well as my own[7]. These are 'ideal types', and any given movement or group will exhibit them in different combinations:

Ideal Types

1. Conservative Islam, best exemplified by the Saudi establishment and well represented throughout the region. Its impetus is primarily to morality and social control. Like conservatism everywhere it enshrines the values of property, family and order (discipline). It is only political in so far as it tries to impose these values through government and law. These elements have always existed, but the rise of the Islamic current gave them a political impetus, in particular the call for the application of the Shari'a. This trend is equally represented in state and official institutions, such as the Azhar and various ministries in Egypt, and the opposition, such as the mainstream of the Muslim Brotherhood.

2. Radical Islam, best exemplified by the Qutbic groups in Egypt. Their aim is the transformation of society by direct action, following the classic injunction to command the good and forbid evil doing (al-*amr bil-ma 'ruf wal-nahy 'anil-munkar*), primarily through the elimination of the un-Islamic ruler, as exemplified by the assassination of Sadat in 1981 and repeated attempts on Mubarak's life and some of his ministers.

3. Political Islam: ideas and programmes of socio-political transformation based on Islam. Best exemplified by some of the Iranian revolutionaries, such as Shari'ati, Talaghani, Bani Sadr and the Mujahidin, and the modernist

elements of the Muslim Brotherhood in Egypt, now split under Hizb al-Wasat. In many respects, this type represents a continuity with nationalist and leftist projects.

How do these types relate to the question of 'democracy'? In the 'charismatic' period, almost all Islamists rejected democracy as an imperialist Western concept alien to Islam. In the case of Iran after the Revolution, they were supported in this view by many sectors of the Left, which has a long history of rejecting 'bourgeois' liberalism. Subsequently, various Islamic voices have played with the idea of democracy, with various interpretations, attributing Islamic lineages to it. One common idea of democracy is that it is the rule of the majority, where an Islamic state is the expression of the will of a Muslim people, a logic with an affinity to many nationalist ideologies. In practice, it is the type 3 political Islamists who are most likely to understand and embrace democratic practice. However, it is important to realise that few Islamists are principled democrats, and in this respect they are not unlike the great majority of political activists of all persuasions in the region. On this issue, it is not so much political convictions that count, but the objective conditions which present constraints and incentives to democratic participation. This is clear in the case of Turkey, where pluralistic electoral competition and the struggle against an entrenched secular establishment makes democracy the most likely game worth playing by the Islamists. And it is a game which engenders forms of organisation and expectations which are difficult to abandon, short of a general collapse of the political system, which is, of course, a possibility.

Iran

Religious institutions in Iran come nearest to the Christian institution of a church separate from the state. This is in contrast to the Sunni countries in the region, constituents then heirs to the Ottoman Empire, in which religion was bureaucratised as a department of state[8]. Iranian religious institutions did not, however, have the centralised and unitary form of, say, the Catholic Church. There is no Pope: every Mujtahid has judicial and spiritual authority for his own followers, and while there is a hierarchy of status, this does not translate into a hierarchy of authority.

Like a Catholic country, Iran is imbued with religion and religious symbols, festivals and ceremonies on the one hand, and a distrust and cynicism towards the clergy on the other. The mourning rituals of Muharram feature public processions, passion plays, organised preaching and chanting which occupy a central part in Shi'i religious and public life. The themes of martyrdom and the commemoration of individual imams, martyrs and holy figures are recurrent features of numerous domestic and public rituals which mark the annual calendar. The pre-Islamic Spring festival of Nowrooz is equally ritualised and endowed with religious symbolism (while held up by the secularists as a liberating pagan occasion). Mosques and shrines define urban and rural landscapes and spaces, and pilgrimage processions are a regular feature of these spaces. In short, time and space in Iran are thoroughly sacralised.

At the same time, more than anywhere else, one can discern a distinct trend to anti-clericalism in modern Iranian history. At the intellectual level there is a degree of continuity from the heterodox 'heresies' of the eighteenth and nineteenth centuries to the secular enlightenment themes of the twentieth. The nineteenth century, on the eve of modernity (later in Iran than the Muslim Mediterranean regions) witnessed doctrinal and social turbulence. Shaykhism, then Babism were charismatic movements which challenged the religious claims and competence of the official clergy in favour of claims of prophethood and mystic gnosis[9]. Persecution and the execution of their leaders drove these movements underground in the form of secret societies. Some of these societies formed the nuclei of subsequent rationalist and modernist ideas and doctrines which entered into the political and cultural struggles of the twentieth century. Anti-clericalism received support, now open, now implicit, from the modernising and secularising thrust of the Pahlavi Shahs. Prominent and popular intellectuals, such as the historical Kasravi, were open critics of the clerical establishment as reactionary and obscurantist[10]. Iranian nationalism constructed its history of the nation with a stress on pre-Islamic glories, and the continuing superiority of Persian culture within Islam, overcoming the barbaric pull from Arabia. These themes, even when not anti-religious, were anti-clerical, and implicitly questioned clerical claims of cultural ascendance. At the popular level we have the stereotype of the molla as hypocritical, venal and grasping, featured in many maxims and jokes. As in Catholic countries, these derogatory stereotypes can be held by many people who are otherwise pious and observant.

The Iranian revolution was not the outcome or an organised Islamic movement[11]. It was, rather, the haphazard result of a conjuncture of factors and forces, many of them not at all religious, such as workers' strikes, and the considerable input from the leftist forces. Religious leadership and organisation came on top largely because religious and bazaar institutions and networks (not political movements) were in place and disposed of funds on a national scale, when no other coherent organisation existed. The thousands or millions brought out on the street were discontented, marginalised recent rural migrants who could identify with the combination of religious and liberationist slogans raised by the revolutionaries, though the rural poor were not distinguished by their piety. Khomeini did acquire a charismatic sanctity fed by messianic expectations. His death and the triumph of the molla state over the revolution changed all that.

The history of political struggles over policy and legislation between the leading factions of the Islamic Republic gives a good picture of the process of 'routinisation', as well as the obstacles to Islamisation in a modern state. The Constitution of the Republic (and its subsequent transformations) is an amalgam of the modern nation state and Islamic principles, such as that of

Khomeini's doctrine of *velayat-i faqih*, the guardianship of the jurist. It enshrines the Shari'a as the privileged source of all legislation (although the Constitution itself is *not* the Shari'a). Yet, ninety percent of legislation is on matters irrelevant to the Shari'a, such as administrative procedures, traffic regulations, economic policies and so on. Faced with this obvious challenge to the inclusiveness of Islam, one leading cleric declared that all these measures were Islamic, in so far as they are not un-Islamic! On controversial issues, such as land reform, labour law and nationalisation of trade, the 1980s were marked by wrangles between conservatives and leftists (within the Islamic field) over the sanctity of private property and freedom of contract, as against public interest and social justice. The matter was partly resolved by Khomeini's famous ruling of 1988, in which he declared that the Islamic government was heir to the authority of the Prophet, and was thus empowered, in the interests of Muslims, to suspend any provisions of the shari'a, including prayer and fasting. In effect this was carte blanche for government to evade the shari'a whenever it suited its interests. This was institutionalised in a Council for the Determination of Public Interest (*tashkhis-I maslahat-I nizam*), thus enshrining the catch-all category of *maslaha*, interest, part of some schools of Sunni fiqh, but historically rejected by the Shi'a, and driving a coach and horses through the Shari'a.

Crucial to the question of the Islamicity of state and society are the laws and rules of family relations and female comportment. Apart from the symbolic and highly visible hejab, which continues to be enforced, the Republic has retreated on many fronts. The Family Protection Laws of the ancien regime were at first denounced as un-Islamic and repealed in favour of the classic Shari'a provisions giving husbands and fathers wide powers (control of wives, renunciation at will, custody, denial of alimony) to the detriment of women and children. Khomeini also ruled that family planning and birth control were forbidden to Muslims, and abolished the programmes initiated by the previous regime, denouncing them as imperialist conspiracies against Islam. Under political pressure from influential Muslim women groups and policy expediency, successive legislative steps more or less restored the provisions of family laws of the ancien regime, giving greater rights and protections to women within marriage, and in social roles[12]. On family planning, Khomeini and the Republic, under threat of one of the highest fertility rates in the world, did a complete about turn and re-started contraception programmes, and a publicity campaign, with posters showing happy families with only two children[13].

These episodes, and many others, induced even greater scepticism among Iranians about Islamic government. A scepticism further enhanced by the political struggles, and the cynical employment of Islamic formulae by the contending parties.

The fragmented authority of the religious institutions were inscribed into the revolutionary state. After Khomeini, no unitary leadership or centre of power prevailed, no Nasser, no Saddam. Different ministries, revolutionary institutions and bonyads (semi-government foundations disposing of great resources) are dominated by various factions and personalities with their own networks and clients. This had its good and bad aspects. Unaccountable powers led to factional strife and corruption. At the same time, the fragmentation of power allowed space for elements of 'civil society' to develop. Repression of dissent was not total, as one side attempted to use it against the other. Ultimately, Rafsanjani's manoeuvring against the conservatives opened up the possibility of a free presidential election in 1997. It was only in the last days of the election campaign that people realised that it was really free, and they voted in great numbers for Khatami against the hard-line Natiq-Nuri, thus inaugurating a new era in Iranian politics, in which liberal and participatory elements can fight the conservatives on more even terms.

In Iran, the country of the popular revolution that became Islamic, there is now a move away from Islamic government. Islamic ideology and institutions, in becoming part of the state and politics, lost their sanctity and charisma. They became embroiled in factional fights and transparently corrupt practices: the negative stereotype of the molla was reinforced. Khomeini's successor as Leader is not distinguished by religious rank or charisma: he was clearly a political appointment. Attempts to make Khamenei a *marja'* have failed. The pious have maintained their allegiance to traditional marja's (authorities), distant from politics.

This is not to say that interest in Islam has necessarily waned. The indications are that there are lively innovations and debates among the younger students and academics of the medreses, including the use of computers for storage and retrieval of texts and fatwas. These include attempts at syntheses between Islamic and Western philosophies and the forging of new social theories and policies. These developments, however, have the effect of distancing Islam from politics and government, in favour of a new Muslim humanism.

These innovations and departures, however, are being strenuously resisted by the conservative (Type 1) forces, led by the senior clerics entrenched in the judiciary, the Majles, sectors of the military (Pasdaran) and the foundations. Reformist forces under Khatami were boosted by the outcome of the parliamentary elections of February 2000, giving them control of the Majles. The struggle continues.

Egypt

Egypt is the country where Islam as an organised political movement started in 1928. This is not to say that this was not preceded by a ferment of ideas and debates, including the notable reforms of the late nineteenth century; but the Muslim Brotherhood was the first movement organising and mobilising followers at a popular level, and which soon developed programmes and strategies[14]. Perhaps this development is related to the early loosening of old communal bonds, at least in Cairo and the north. The economic and political transformations and upheavals of the nineteenth century included migrations and the decline of traditional crafts and sources of livelihood. Sufi *turuq*, the main form of popular religious organisation, had been superimposed on craft guilds and urban quarters, and declined with them. This is very different from Iran where bazaar and guild networks, with their religious components, continued as important forms of popular association until much later in the twentieth century and in some respects till the present time. The Muslim Brotherhood, then, stepped into this vacuum and provided means of popular associations and piety, with a political strategy in relation to the semi-colonial subordination of Egypt at the time. In the first half of the century, with Egypt featuring a plurality of power centres and political forces, the MB was one political force amongst many, liberal, left and nationalist parties; but all, in one way or another, seeking national independence.

The Nasserist revolution and the unitary state it inaugurated put an end to that pluralism. The MB was suppressed alongside other parties, and its sometimes violent resistance brought about intensified persecution. In any case, Islamist appeal waned in the heyday of Nasserism, lasting till 1967, which enjoyed overwhelming popular sentiment. Nasserist land reforms and welfare provisions acted as a social cement attaching the people to the state. It was the defeat of Nasserism in the 1967 war with Israel, then its collapse under Sadat, which opened the way for renewed political activity and the revival of forms of Islamism. Besides, it is well known that Sadat in his struggle against Nasserists and the left encouraged and fostered Islamic activism.

Political liberalisation in Egypt under Sadat and Mubarak was always limited, and recently suffered many reverses. A number of political parties were licensed, (but not religious parties), with newspapers and candidates in parliamentary elections. A limited freedom of the press was allowed, as well as opposition and public debate (now ever more restricted). Any attempt, however, for parties to organise and mobilise a popular constituency is resisted, and parliamentary elections are largely a show run by the government which allows a small, and ever decreasing, number of seats for opposition parties. The dominant government party is no more than a vehicle of loyalty and patronage for the President and the political directorate, while opposition parties are little more than clubs and talking shops. The only political forces organised at the popular level are Islamist groups, although they are not licensed parties, and their organisation is largely based on 'social Islam', the network of charities, services and employment opportunities offered by Muslim associations and companies, an important consequence of the withdrawal of the state from welfare provision.

What, then is the current position of political Islam in Egypt? The radical Islamists, the direct action and sometimes violent groups such as Jihad and Gama'at Islamiyya, occupied centre stage, at least in public and media consciousness through their dramatic acts and bizarre, initially almost messianic ideology. Although small in numbers, they managed at the height of their power in the 1980s to rule whole communities in Upper

Egypt as well as popular Cairo quarters, notably 'Ain Shams and Imbaba, by a mixture of conviction and intimidation[15]. They instituted communalist authoritarianism, emphasising morality and discipline. They engaged in a long and continuing battle with the government which brought the full and considerable weight of the security services upon them in a wave of intense and indiscriminate repression. It seems that the authorities have won, and these groups are now much diminished and in disarray, the Gama'at declaring a truce and acknowledging failure of its direct action.

The Muslim Brotherhood is split mostly along generational lines. The older generation is conservative in the sense indicated in Type 1, to which I shall return. The younger generation, of cadres in their 40s, the generation of the student struggles of the 1970s, many of whom subsequently became leading figures in the professional syndicates taken over by Islamists in the 80s and early 90s, are of Type 3, true political Islamists with a programme continuous with the nationalist project. They are currently engaged in a legal struggle with the government over licensing a new political party, Hizb al-Wasat, the Centre Party. They have been refused at every step, on the grounds that their programme is already covered by existing parties. The MB leadership has openly opposed the foundation of this party.

The political Islamists (Type 3) above, as exemplified by Hizb al-Wasat, have programmes of economic and social policies, mostly in historical continuity with the 'national project' of Nasserism and the left. Resistance to dependency on the world market and global capitalism, economic planning, social justice and welfare, are all issues which this type of political Islam shares with the nationalists and leftists. Activists in this strand emphasise common social action and national unity between all patriotic forces, and to that end campaign for extension of democracy and a free political field. It is significant that the petitioners for the foundation of Hizb al-Wasat included Coptic personalities. The authorities, as we have seen, have rejected the application of this party for a license. The leaders of this trend of oppositional political Islam are currently under considerable pressure, with many arrests (belonging to an illegal organisation), trials and general harassment. This is consistent with the government's resistance to any extension of opposition forces and activity, and their restriction of the scope of democracy and representation. This leaves the Islamic field clear for conservative Islam (Type 1 above), and the increasingly convergent radical Islam (Type 2).

Radical Islam shares many ideological features with the conservatives. The two are different in their social constituencies and modes of action. Radical Islam, as we saw, calls for direct action against what it considers to be un-Islamic government and a *jahili* society. Its constituency is predominantly poor and young. The Jihad and the Jama'at Islamiyya engaged in waves of violence against the government, the police, tourists and public personalities opposed to the Islamic current or condemned by it for apostasy or unbelief, such as the writer Farag Foda, assassinated in 1992, and the attempt on the life of the famous novelist Naguib Mahfouz soon after. The concerted campaign of repression by the authorities against those groups and their social supports (neighbourhoods, villages and communities) has been largely successful. Violence and direct action have subsided, and the militants have settled down in particular quarters and communities where they instituted regimes of authoritarian morality and forced observance. This is the point of their convergence with conservative Islam.

Conservative Islam has its constituency in more prosperous and influential social locations: businessmen, lawyers, functionaries and ulama. Their social programme is conceived in moral and ritual terms: to enforce moral conduct in accordance with religious precepts, and to that end to combat and reject alien imports of social cultural models. Rituals of prayer, fasting and 'purity' in sexual and other bodily functions are enjoined. The Shari'a is to be enforced in all matters. A totalised Islam of religion, society, government and culture is opposed to an equally totalised 'West', conceived in religious terms as Christian, but secularised, corrupt and in decline[16]. In all these respects they converge with the radicals. But the conservative emphasis on the values of property and order lead them to reject the violence and insubordination of the radicals. This rejection of violence, however, is not consistent, as some ulama have expressed sympathy for the radical sentiments and motives while rejecting their methods, and some have attempted to mediate between the violent groups and the authorities. One direction of violence which does not elicit condemnation, but often support, is when its targets are anti-Islamic intellectuals. In the trial of the killers of Farag Foda, a prominent cleric, Muhammad al-Ghazzali testified in court that it was legitimate in Islam to kill apostates.

The political advocacy of conservative Islam is predominantly ethical and disciplinary. Its economic policy consists in the banning of *riba*, dealing in interest. It considers all other forms of capitalist activity legitimate. Indeed, the business sector is a favoured field for its activities. Financial scandals surrounded the Islamic investment companies in the 1980s: the companies, arising mostly from financial transfers from migrant workers in the Gulf and escaping government regulation, offered huge returns on deposits. This was a share of the profits rather than interest, and was rumoured to stem from speculation in gold and financial markets, as well as paying existing depositors from new deposits. Most of them collapsed when the government moved in to regulate them. Their defenders included many leading ulama, like Shaykh Sha'rawi, and others who declared them part of Egyptian and Muslim authenticity in traditional financial dealings[17].

The only opposition that conservative Islamism may offer to the government is in terms of its failure to enforce the legal and moral commands of religion, and its tolerance of Western and other non-Islamic elements in education and cultural fields. Some may also oppose aspects of foreign policy, such as relations with America and especially Israel. Such opposition does come from elements in the mainstream Muslim Brotherhood, and from some independent clerics. At the same time, the authorities have succeeded in co-opting conservative Islam in its institutions and media.

Until quite recently, official Islam of the leading ulama and the institution of al-Azhar, was largely subordinate to government, issuing fatwas to legitimate whatever was current policy. Radical Islamists have always been highly critical of the ulama on these counts, and regarded them as part of *jahili* society. A transformation has occurred since the 1980s, with the government increasingly reliant on the ulama to establish its own Islamic credentials against religious opposition. Sadat wrote into the Egyptian constitution that the Shari'a was the main source of all legislation (which is in contradiction to the actual content of Egyptian positive law). This gave the ulama, custodians of the Shari'a greater confidence. Not to be outdone by the increasingly prominent advocacy of political Islam, the ulama ventured into the political field with their own platforms, often supported by the state and its institutions. Al-Azhar has emerged as the main defender of religious orthodoxy, claiming to itself the right to monitor and censor all cultural and intellectual products, not just the religious. Al-Azhar is a complex institution with different, and sometimes conflicting, organs. Under the previous Rector, Jad al-Haqq (d. 1996), the institution moved to the right, and its organs, such as the Committee for Research and Publication claimed the power (endorsed by some state organs) to censor cultural products. The Front of Azhar Ulama has also been active in monitoring and condemning persons, products and events in the name of orthodoxy. The new Rector, Shaykh Tantawi, a more liberal figure, has been at odds with these committees, which continue to be active and vociferous[18]. Informal groups, such as the Muslim Lawyers Association, are also active in prosecuting writers, film makers and cinema owners for un-Islamic products or indecent displays (cinema posters). This was the group behind the prosecution of Nasir Hamid Abu-Zayd, an academic who wrote critical books on issues in religion and the Quran, to divorce him from his Muslim wife, on the grounds of his supposed apostasy (a Muslim woman cannot be married to a non-Muslim). This was their way of getting a court to declare Abu-Zayd and apostate, given that there is no such charge in Egyptian law[19].

Conservative clerics can propagate their message through radio and television, with considerable broadcasting time devoted to religious themes. These include explication of the correct performance of ritual and bodily purity, as well as the tortures of the grave for those of deficient faith and observance.

We see then that conservative Islam spans government and opposition, with an overlap between the two. Many state personnel and organs are sympathetic to its message and include its personnel. The legal system is increasingly exploitable by Islamic lawyers for their moralistic and censoring purposes. But there is also resistance from some religious and state elements, such as the liberal Rector of Al-Azhar, and the official government censor, jealous of the usurpation of his powers by religious bodies. The legality of these various steps is ambiguous. The overall effect, however, is unmistakable: the increasing Islamisation of Egyptian society and culture, with the acquiescence, if not the support, of a pious and compliant population, resentful of the blatant displays of wealth (often in Western styles) by the elites, in the middle of their own poverty.

Turkey

The 'secular' Turkish Republic is imbued and obsessed with religion. Turkish identity and proper citizenship in the Republic coincides with Sunni Islam, not necessarily as religious practice, but as communal identity. The traumatic struggles in the formation of the Republic were against enemies who were religiously identified (Greek, Armenian and the European powers), and the emergent secular Kemalist Republic was implicitly Muslim. Turkish nationalism embraced this identity, and Turkish Islam emerged as nationalist Islam[20].

Kemalism as a secular and Europeanised identity was and is restricted to important but minority sectors of the Istanbul and Ankara bourgeoisie, political, professional and media elites. The mass of Kemalists, ardent nationalists and subscribers to its statist and secularist doctrines are at the same time good Muslims. Strong Islamo-nationalist sentiments distinguish many of the leading cadres and politicians of the main parties, not only the openly sympathetic Motherland Party under Ozal in the 1980s and early 90s, but also the True Path Party of President Dimirel. That is in addition to the openly Islamic Refah/Fazilet Party. Government departments and ministries, quite apart from the vast Religious Affairs Directorate, include many functionaries and managers with Islamic affiliations (education, interior, now being purged).

Ataturk sought to subordinate religion to the state and the nationalist project. This project was directed to 'progress' conceived in terms of European models of modernity. If Turkey was to become a European state and nation, all 'oriental' elements had to be jettisoned or suppressed. Religion was to be purified from its 'backward' elements and Turkified. A dress code was imposed for religious personnel, which substituted a beret for the turban; the call to prayer was henceforth to be chanted in Turkish; the Arabic script was abolished in favour of the Latin. Most important, the Sufi orders, the most common forms of popular religiosity and association, were interdicted and suppressed. In this respect Ataturk shared the zeal for religious 'purity' of the Muslim reformers and the Wahhabis. Religious foundations, education and worship were all subsumed under a state department, what was to become the Religious Affairs Directorate.

Religion, however, continued to feature prominently in the life of many Turks, and its expressions and organization to develop in the shadow of Kemalism. One of the most potent social constituencies which maintained its religious outlook was the provincial urban bourgeoisie of merchants, craftsmen and functionaries. Ataturk's one-party state was ended in 1950, with the installation of two-party electoral competition. The provincial constituency was strongly represented in the opposition Democrat Party which succeeded in the early elections[21]. The Democrat government reversed some of the Kemalist excesses, notably the restoration of the call to prayer in Arabic, and relaxation of the dress code for the religious classes. As multi-party competition advanced, more conservative Muslim elements were included in the mainstream parties, until the present time, when there are strong Muslim representations in the two parties of the right. The Motherland Party is particularly interesting, because its founder and chief in the 1980s, Turgut Ozal (d. 1993), came from the religious milieu of the Sufi order of the Nakshibandis, as were many members of his entourage who formed the first elected government after the 1981 military coup. Ozal brought extensive reforms to the economy, in line with the structural re-adjustment which started on a world-wide scale at the time. But he also attempted to liberalise state and society, instituting a much greater degree of religious freedom, which saw the flourishing of Muslim foundations and religious schools. These schools are known as *Imam-Hatip*, for the training of religious personnel, but became, in fact, a parallel education system which combined religious studies with a regular curriculum. Some of them became elite schools, sending graduates to the best university faculties, leading, in turn, to high positions in government, business and the professions. Ozal's demise in 1993 ushered in a new leadership for his party with none of his vision or charisma, and one which reverted to Kemalist orthodoxy. Many of the Muslim elements left the Motherland Party, some joining the renovated pro-Islamic Refah Party.

The predecessor of the Refah party, under the same leader, Erbakan, came on to the political stage in the 1970s, the decade of intense conflict and violent confrontation between Left and Right. At that point the National Salvation Party, as it was known then, was firmly identified with the Right, and entered into local alliances and joint activities with the ultra-nationalist (some would say Fascist) party of Turkes, of Grey Wolf fame (now the National Movement Party, a junior partner in the current government coalition). Ultra-nationalism and Sunni Muslim activism were superimposed on one another in a violent confrontation with the left, in turn comprising a strong Alevi (heterodox Muslim) presence. At one point in the late 1970s, the chaos of political upheaval and a fragmented parliament brought the Islamic party into coalition government with a multiplicity of parties. Its share of the spoils was a strong representation of its cadres and right-wing allies in the ministries of education and the interior, one that continues till the present (though more recently subject to a purge dictated by the military).

The restoration of democracy after the 1981 military coup saw the resurgence of the Islamic party under its new name of Refah, Welfare (to be changed yet again after its recent indictment to Fazilet, Virtue). As we saw, it benefitted from the fall out from the Motherland Party after Ozal died. In 1994 it won control of the municipalities of Istanbul, Ankara and several other major cities, and in 1996 parliamentary elections, it came out as the largest party (but only marginally, with 23 per cent of the votes), and entered into coalition with the Right Path Party in government. These successes rang the alarm bells for the secular establishment, led by the military top brass. Under their pressure and intimidation, the coalition fell, and legal steps were taken against the Party and its leaders, accused of subverting the secular Constitution, and culminating in the interdiction of the Party (reformed under the new name) and in banning its leader Erbakan from political participation. In the last parliamentary election in 1999 the Party lost its lead and came third after the Ecevit's Democratic Left and the ultra-nationalist National Movement parties, now in coalition government. It shows, at least, that religious appeal in a competitive electoral system can rise and fall following circumstances. Events on the Kurdish front, including the dramatic capture and trial of Ocalan gave the ultra-nationalists an issue of considerable popular appeal. In any case, as we saw, there is a considerable overlap between the ultra-nationalist and the Islamic constituencies, even though the parties themselves have drifted apart, a testimony to the interweaving between Islam and Turkish nationalism.

The 'incubation' of Islam under Kemalist interdictions and its later resurgence, has many cultural and institutional dimensions besides the political. Sufi orders were a dominant feature of Turkish religious life for much of Ottoman history. Their suppression under Ataturk drove them underground and deprived them from popular appeal and participation. Some of them, however, were transformed in the process, adapting to the conditions of modernity, to emerge as major players in social, cultural as well as political life.

We have already noted the Nakshibandi order and its input into politics at the time of Ozal. Elements from this order were also instrumental in the foundation and functioning of the Refah/Fazilet party (Erbakan is said to come from that milieu). But perhaps the most prominent religious movement is that of the Nurcu. It was founded by one Said Nursi, a contemporary of Ataturk, and at first a supporter, who came from a Sufi Kurdish milieu[23]. However, Nursi had the foresight to guess that traditional Sufi organisation, often local and depending on personalist networks, was inappropriate for modern societies and nation states. His organization was to engage in the dissemination of religious knowledge and piety through the printed word, and an engagement with modern life, including science. This organisation was to survive Kemalist repression and to grow in adherence and wealth, and to emerge in recent times as one of the most potent elements in Turkish society. Its major modern off-shoot is known as 'Fethullacilar', after its prominent leader Fethulla Gulen. It disposes of considerable resources in wide ranging activities. In education, it founded many schools with, reputedly, high standards of education, especially in the sciences and in foreign languages. It also features student hostels and dispenses scholarships for higher eduction. Its educational activities extend to Turkish communities abroad, and to former Soviet republics. It recently opened a private university, the first such to be founded by a religious organisation. In the media, it owns Zaman, a mainstream respectable conservative daily, and a TV channel, and publishes many books, pamphlets and magazines. It is constituted as a *vakif*, a foundation: these are instituted under a Turkish law of foundations, promulgated in the 1980s, which closely follows the American law on the subject. Fethulla himself, while ostensibly shunning politics, has access to the President, the Prime Minister and other prominent political personalities, and is treated as a guru. Secularist Turks are, naturally, suspicious of these activities. In recent months, a campaign was started in the media against Fethulla and his organization accusing them of infiltrating the state, attempting to infiltrate the army and plotting to take over the country. This is part of the secularist backlash against growing religious manifestations in politics, society and culture. Regardless of the outcome of the current struggles, however, these religious elements have become embedded in Turkish society, and can only be eliminated with considerable repression and violence.

The Turkish Republic is not a liberal democracy, and its human rights and rule of law records are well known. However, it does have a genuinely pluralistic parliamentary system, with alternation of governments in accordance with majorities (interrupted by periodic military takeovers, but always restored), and in this respect quite unlike any other country in the region except Israel.

Two factors stand out in shaping the trajectory of Turkish Islam in contrast to other countries in the region: its struggle against a powerful and appealing secular elite entrenched in government, education and the media; and the fact of a competitive electoral system, reinforced from the 1980s with a freer and plural institutional and associational life, including municipal government, private broadcasting and autonomous foundations. These factors set it apart from Egypt, Iran and practically all other countries in the region.

In terms of our typology of Islamism, we can discern a numerical and cultural dominance of Type 1 conservative Islam: the provincial bourgeoisie and the dominant sectors of the reconstituted orders and foundations fall within category, and are represented in the Islamic party by Erbakan and his generation and circle. Type 3 political Muslims are also represented in the Islamic party by the younger generation (in their 40s) exemplified by Recep Erdogan, the colourful, now impeached, Mayor of Istanbul. They are a generation who grew up politically in the milieu of the parties of the Left, often fighting against them, but also learning from their methods and programmes. Groups of prominent Islamic intellectuals and poets have affinities to this generation. The Type 2 radicals are a marginal and unimportant group in Turkish Islam: they are foreshadowed and swamped by right-wing ultra-nationalist radicalism and violence. Qutbist or Iranian-style radical Islamists exist, but constitute small and fragmented groups with little impact.

Conservative Islamists, however, are driven by the peculiar Turkish conditions to be much more political and open than their Egyptian or other Arab counterparts. They cannot openly advocate the application of the Shari'a because, apart from being an offence in Turkish law, it would not go down very well with important sectors of the electorate, notably middle class women. Electoral competition exacts its price on ideological purity. Further, political conservatives must have a social and economic programme beyond ethical proclamations and moral disciplines: they are driven into the territory of Type 3 politicals, and also come up with garbled and diluted versions of old leftist economics dressed up in Islamic terms.

Turkey, because of its highly developed and pluralistic institutional and associational life, as well as its political field and organisation, has featured an Islam which is much more public and institutional outside the strictly religious locations than in Egypt and most of the Arab world which, because of the limitations on politics and public life, give rise to more private and communal association (also, of course, present in Turkey as in most parts of the world). In this context, Islam becomes one element amongst many in political and public life and is involved in the contest of ideas and interests, much like Christian democracy in Europe. However, the current attempts to restrict and limit any form of dissent in Turkey and the specific attack on public Islam threatens this peaceful development.

Conclusion

I have tried to show how the trajectories of development of political Islam in the three countries follow the contours of their respective histories and political cultures. After the initial 'charismatic' period of Islamic resurgence in the 1970s and early 90s, Islamic movements have become integrated into the politics of their respective contexts and 'routinised' into modes of operation and adjustment to that context. There are, of course, common elements, as we have noted, such as the contest between conservative and political forms of Islamism. I should also add one important common dilemma to all Islamism: the secularisation of their societies and cultures.

The Islamic thrust in recent decades has been in large part a reaction against secularisation and its ostensible aim was to stop and reverse that process. It succeeded in this respect in many visible ways: veiling of women and segregation of the sexes; the interdiction of alcohol; the prohibition (in practice re-shaping) of interest on loans; and in the case of Egypt and Iran, the introduction of the Shari'a, in different ways, into the legal system. But have these measures halted the inexorable socio-economic processes which are difficult to control or plan? Take the question of women and the family. It was the stated aim of all Islamic movements to keep women at home as mothers and home-makers, the cornerstone of the Muslim family. Yet everywhere women are going out of the home to work in ever increasing numbers. Families cannot afford home-bound mothers, and the occupational structure offers increasing opportunities. Paradoxically, the veil has facilitated rather than inhibited this much wider social and economic participation by women, in bestowing respectability and modesty on female public appearance. Or take the example of women's political participation: one of the planks of Khomeini's rise against the ancien regime in 1963 was in opposition to the granting of political rights to women, including the vote. Yet, at the inception of the Islamic Republic, there was no question of not granting women these rights. In Egypt, and other Arab lands, it is only the most backward conservatives who object to women's political participation, and they are losing. We have seen the about-turn of the Iranian regime on family law and family planning in the face of modern sensibilities and pragmatic considerations. I have noted Khomeini's ruling in 1988, authorising the bypassing of the Shari'a in favour of the interests of Islamic government. This is the clearest step in the direction of pragmatism, opening the gates wide for adjusting policy and legislation to current imperatives. In the area of crime and punishment, it is noted that although the Shari'a penalties are on the law books in Iran, they are seldom applied, and then for political motives. These are applied in Saudi Arabia, with a society largely controlled by the constraints and incentives of a petrolic authoritarianism, and even then the victims are predominantly foreign workers without rights. Afghanistan is a society thoroughly devastated and fragmented by continuous warfare, and offers little resistance to the strict enforcement of a literal Shari'a.

The greatest challenge to the Shari'a, however, is not the push for the modifications of its provisions and applications, but the fact that it is just *irrelevant* to the great bulk of legislation in a modern society. We have seen how one cleric in Iran, in admitting this fact, covered it with the statement that so long as it did not contradict Shari'a provisions, legislation on practical affairs of administration and policy was 'not un-Islamic'.

The media is another area of the incursion of ideas and processes which cannot be controlled. It is interesting, first of all, that efforts to ban or severely restrict film, TV and music in Saudi Arabia then in Iran, failed, and these media were incorporated into Islamic states with various degrees of control. The Internet poses the most potent challenge for all censorship regimes. Of course, the Islamic forces were very quick to adopt these media, often with great success, in propagating their messages. Yet, there are unintended consequences which are not that positive. The multiplicity of religious voices which enter the contest for authority of enunciation on the many different sites, especially on the Internet, do not only confuse and challenge sources of traditional religious authority, but also 'banalize' religion, by offering it alongside entertainment and shopping: the sacred is denuded of its mystery and awe by rubbing shoulders with the profane. Control over the message and its context is slipping from the sources of authority in government and religious institutions, and censorship is becoming ever more difficult. Internet cafes are now widespread in Tehran.

It is against these processes and forces which they cannot control that voices of religious authority are ever more vociferous in denunciation, especially the Type 1 conservatives. Are they fighting a losing battle?

Finally, a word on 'trans-national' Islam. I have here presented political Islam as being integrated into national histories and cultures. Is this contradicted by the well known international manifestations of that religion? The question of trans-national Islam is important and interesting, and will need another paper to tackle it. For the purpose of the present discussion I would argue that these international manifestations are developing in parallel, and with some interaction with national developments. For the most part they are institutionally and organisationally separate. One sector of international Islam is a consequence of the Afghan wars and still proceedings within the Afghan networks. It includes Arabs and Pakistanis, but is, for the most part, separate from the national political scenes in Egypt and elsewhere. It is interesting to note that, through the Turkish Diaspora, Islamic parties and institutions have established networks in Europe and elsewhere which are specifically Turkish and do not mix with Muslims of other nationalities. In addition, there are developments of Islamic ideas and organisations in the Muslim communities of Europe and America, and these are potentially the most creative, because they are developing in liberal political settings.

Notes

1 Max Weber, *Economy and Society*, New York, Bedminister, 1968, pp. 241–54, 1111–56.

2 There is an ambiguity in Weber's concept of charisma: at first it seems to attach to a person as a leader, but is subsequently used to designate ideas and communities as, for example, in his treatment of Protestantism. See discussion in Ralph Schroeder, *Max Weber and the Sociology of Culture*, London, Sage, 1992, pp. 17–23.

3 On Sayyid Qutb and the radical groups who pursued his doctrines, see Giles Kepel, *The Prophet and the Pharaoh: Muslim Extremism in Egypt*, London, Al-Saqi, 1985; and Sami Zubaida, *Islam, the People and the State*, Second edition, London, Tauris, 1993, pp. 51–5.

4 For an analysis of this discourse, see Sami Zubaida, *op. cit.*, and Yann Richard, *Shi'ite Islam: Polity, Ideology and Creed*, Oxford, Blackwell, 1995.

5 Olivier Roy, *The Failure of Political Islam*, London, Tauris, 1994.

6 Asghar Schirazi, *The Constitution of Iran: Politics and the State in the Islamic Republic*, London, Tauris, 1997.

7 Nazih Ayubi, *Political Islam: Religion and Politics in the Arab World*, London, Routledge, 1991; Olivier Roy, *op. cit.*, Sami Zubaida, 1993, *op. cit.*

8 For a comparison of Iran with Egypt in these respects, see Sami Zubaida, 1993, *op. cit.*, pp. 38–73.

9 Mangol Bayat, *Mysticism and Dissent: Socio-religious Thought in Qajar Iran*, Syracuse, 1992.

10 Ervand Abrahamian, 'Kasravi: the Integrative Nationalist of Iran', in *Middle East Studies*, 9:3, 1973, pp. 271–95.

11 Asaf Bayat, 'Revolution without Movement, Movement without Revolution: Comparing Islamic Activism in Iran and Egypt', *Comparative Studies in Society and History*, 40:1, 1988, pp. 136–69.

12 Sami Zubaida, 'Is Iran an Islamic State?', in J. Beinin and J. Stork eds., *Political Islam: Essays from Middle East Report*, Berkeley, University of California Press, 1997, pp. 103–19.

13 Homa Hodfar, 'Devices and Desires: Population Policy and Gender Roles in the Islamic Republic', in J. Beinin and J. Stork, eds., *op. cit.*, pp. 220–33.

14 R. P. Mitchell, *The Society of Muslim Brothers*, Oxford, OUP, 1969.

15 Salwa Ismail, 'The Politics of Urban Cairo: Informal Communities and the State', *Arab Studies Journal*, Fall, 1996, pp. 119–32.

16 For an analysis of the discourses of conservative Islamism, see Salwa Ismail, 'Confronting the Other Identity, Culture, Politics and Conservative Islamism in Egypt', *International Journal of Middle East Studies*, 30, 1998, pp. 199–225.

17 Alan Roussillon, *Societes islamiques de placement de fonds et 'ouvertures economique'*, Cairo, Dossiers du CEDEI, 1988; Sami Zubaida, 'The Politics of the Islamic Investment Companies in Egypt', *Bulletin of the British Society for Middle East Studies*, 17:2, 1990, pp. 152–61.

18 Salwa Ismail, 'Religious "Orthodoxy" and Public Morality: the State, Islamism and Cultural Politics in Egypt', *Critique*, Spring 1999, pp. 152–61.

19 Baudouin Dupret, 'Le proces l'augmentation des tribunaux', *Monde Arabe: Maghreb Machrek*, 151, 1996, pp. 18–21.

20 See Sami Zubaida, 'Turkish Islam and National Identity', *Middle East Report*, 26:2, 1996, pp. 10–15.

21 Eric Zurcher, *Modern Turkey*, London, Tauris, 1993.

22 Serif Mardin, *Religion and Social Change in Modern Turkey: the Case of Bediuzzaman Said Nursi*, Albany, SUNY Press, 1989.

American Fundamentalism and the Selling of God

HAROLD PERKIN

AMERICAN religious fundamentalism, like American religious practice as a whole, is *sui generis*. As the Mansfield College Conference on Religion and Democracy worldwide showed, it conforms to no other kind in the world. Its relation to globalisation on the capitalist model is paradoxical, to say the least. If we accept the thesis that the rise of fundamentalism in the Third World is a reaction against the marginalising and cultural disorientation forced on politically weak, economically impoverished, and psychologically demoralised people by the post-imperialistic West, it is obvious that the American Christian Right are a very different case. They enjoy political power, living standards, and freedom of expression far better than most of the non-Western world. They have all the benefits of globalisation without, it seems, the costs. Yet its adherents—not, I hasten to say, their leaders whose interests are quite different, as we shall see—are in a curious way just as much victims, though luckier and less exploited, as their Third World counterparts.

Fundamentalism I take to be more than a profound belief in God (or Gods). It is the conviction that the adherents have a special knowledge of and relationship to a Deity, based either on a sacred and unquestionable text or on direct contact with and experience of God's message. This allows or even enjoins imposing what they take to be God's will upon other people and, if necessary, punishing them for their disbelief. It therefore overrides any appeal to a secular authority, notably to the will of the majority, and thus to democratic sovereignty. If they cannot persuade a political majority to support them, they claim to have the religious or moral majority, the majority of true believers or of those with supreme values and God's blessing. In extreme cases, as in the European middle ages or contemporary Afghanistan and the Sudan, this can mean imposing capital punishment for apostasy or moral offences such as adultery or abortion. It is what I have called elsewhere 'the tyranny of the virtual majority'[1]. Fundamentalist religion, therefore, is at odds with democracy as ordinarily understood.

The word fundamentalism itself, it seems, was first used in its religious sense in the United States in 1920, in the course of a dispute within conservative Protestantism, to distinguish between those who believed that the Bible was the word of God dictated to his prophets and scribes, and those who allowed it was by human hands merely inspired by God, and therefore potentially subject to errors of transmission and translation. The label was worn proudly by the first group, and later transformed into 'Evangelicalism' (meaning, paradoxically as it turns out, belief in the Gospels rather than the

© The Political Quarterly Publishing Co. Ltd. 2000
Published by Blackwell Publishers, 108 Cowley Road, Oxford OX4 1JF, UK and 350 Main Street, Malden, MA 02148, USA

Old Testament) by Billy Graham and his fellow preachers in the late 1950s. Later, largely in the 1970s and 1980s, it was taken over by the 'New Christian Right', who attempted to unite the conservative Protestants into a powerful lobby with intent to press their agenda on to the Republican Party under Presidents Nixon, Reagan and Bush[2].

The New Christian Right have, since President Richard Nixon's time, claimed to be 'the moral majority' of the American people. Nixon spoke of 'the silent majority', those who upheld 'the traditional values of middle-class Americans—hard work, individual enterprise, orderly behavior, love of country, moral piety, and material progress'[3]. The subtext, of course, was that these were not the values of his opponents, particularly those who opposed his neo-colonial war in Vietnam, the bombing of Cambodia, and his nefarious electioneering tactics in the Watergate affair. His friend the Rev. Jerry Falwell seized on this and turned it into the 'Moral Majority, Inc.' founded in 1979, the year before his friend Ronald Reagan's election as President.

In that year Falwell launched his 'Clean Up America' campaign, and told its 20 million viewers and listeners: 'We are the "moral majority" and we have been silent long enough.' He appealed to 'the simple faith on which this country was built,' which was in danger from liberals, abortionists, drug dealers, homosexuals, and—significantly—critics of capitalism and the Cold War[4]. This latter placed him on the far bank from the fundamentalists of the Third World. He and his Evangelical allies, televangelist preachers like Pat Robertson, Oral Roberts, Jim and Tammy Bakker, Jimmy Swaggart, and later Ralph Reed of the Christian Coalition, all embraced the political dogma of the Republican Party (and indeed of most Democrats): the free market, corporate power, the right of multinationals to trade and invest everywhere on the world, in short all the forces of globalisation on the American big business model. On the face of it, nothing could be further from non-American fundamentalists' reaction to global capitalism and opposition to Western corporate domination of the world economy than the Christian Right.

In this article I want to address three questions:
1) Was the Christian Right anywhere near a political majority of the American people, or merely a minority on the religious wing of the Republican Party?
2) Was it in effect a part of big business, a segment of the services sector, making profits by 'Selling God' (to quote the title of one contemporary study), and turning its CEOs into multi-millionaires?
3) Despite this, did its followers have different motives and fears from the leaders, and were they reacting against some at least of the deleterious side-effects of American capitalism?

The Weight of the Christian Right

Organised religion in the United States is on a larger scale than elsewhere in the West. Americans claim to be more religious in the sense of church-going than any other people, except perhaps in miniscule Malta. Sixty per cent are enrolled as members of a church or synagogue, and 40 per cent attend a place of worship in a typical week—compared with 14 per cent in Britain and 12 per cent in France. Nine out of ten express belief in God, eight in ten believe in the New Testament miracles, and expect to meet their maker on the Day of Judgment. Only seven in ten believe in life after death, so one in those eight must think they will not pass the test. Five in ten believe in angels, and four in ten in a personal devil. Only three Americans in a hundred admit to disbelief in God. Garry Wills, doyen of presidential historians, points out that no non-Christian has ever been elected to that high office, no Catholic until John F. Kennedy in 1960, and the idea of an atheist, as distinct from a sinner, in the White House is unthinkable[5].

Americans are far more censorious of 'sin' than Europeans. To most of them it means sexual transgression rather than financial corruption: they are very cynical about the honesty of politicians but still vote for them. Adultery by French presidents like Giscard d'Estaing or Francois Mitterrand, or by British politicians like Cecil Parkinson or David Mellor, seems only to have enhanced their careers; but Gary Hart's affair with Donna Rice did prevent, and Bill Clinton's numerous alleged assignations had they become known in time would have prevented, their election. The legacy of the Puritans, including their prurience and hypocrisy, is still strong, as the current media-raking over of George Bush Junior's past bears witness.

According to opinion polls in the 1980s, 70 per cent of American Protestants and 71 per cent of Catholics believe that 'adultery is always wrong', though only 46 per cent of the more tolerant Jews (only 2 per cent of believers, however)[6]. These views are enshrined in state law. Adultery is illegal in most American states: in most of New England, right across the South, and in California, Kansas, Nebraska, Nevada (of the Reno 'quickie divorce'), and Utah (where some Mormon dissidents still boast of practising polygamy). Oral sex, even between married couples, is illegal in twenty-three states, and is punishable as 'sodomy' in Georgia, where it is alleged to be ex-Speaker Newt Gingrich's 'alternative to adultery' (*World Press Review*, September 1977). Fortunately, these laws are rarely enforced, or by common opinion Congress and the White House would be decimated. And, as the best-selling Starr Report on President Clinton's involvement with 'Whitewater' and unrelated matters culminating in sex with Monica Lewinski shows, American prurience over sex in high places has escalated since Roosevelt's, Eisenhower's and Kennedy's well-known but media ignored affairs.

The polls also show that, much more than income, class or race, religion remains one of the most accurate, and least appreciated, political indicators available. The religious lobbies of all persuasions ensure that the politicians at least appreciate it. Billy Graham (voted 'the most admired man in America', along with Pope John Paul II and Rev. Jesse Jackson) has been the friend of every American President since Eisenhower except for the Catholic Kennedy and the erring Clinton. Despite the separation of church and state,

Eisenhower wrote God into government for the first time, with prayers at his inauguration, a national day of prayer, 'One Nation under God' in the Pledge of Allegiance, and 'In God We Trust' on the paper currency. Nixon made Graham his special adviser, who told him to ignore the Catholics in his 1960 campaign (which he consequently lost).

Kennedy's relations with Rome were mutually beneficial, as his family's marriage annulments testify. Jimmy Carter, though a 'born again' Christian, confessed in *Playboy* to 'adultery in his heart'. Reagan, a 'born again' divorcee, embraced the Christian Right. They trumpeted in 1980 that 'Our time is come.' Televangelist Pat Robertson boasted, 'We have enough votes to run the country . . . we are going to take over.' Even the cool, unemotional George Bush was convinced by the adulterous, bisexual Jim Bakker that 'born again' meant only accepting Christ as his saviour (*New York Review of Books*, 29 May 1997, p. 30). The confessed sinner Bill Clinton gave the charismatic builder of the $40 million dollar Crystal Cathedral, Robert Schuller the place of honour beside the First Lady at his second inauguration (*Newsweek*, 3 May 1997).

All this might suggest that the loudest spokesmen for religion have the most influence in American politics, and ought to carry the majority of voters with them. Yet all the opinion polls show that they fall far short of a majority. One test is their opposition to abortion, with some devotees bombing clinics and murdering doctors. This is condemned by a clear majority of American women who favour the right to choose. Statistics of self-expressed beliefs all undermine the Christian Right's claim to dominate public opinion. According to a Gallup poll in 1980, at the peak of their influence, 'born again' Christians were no more than 19 per cent of the national sample, 22 per cent of women and only 15 per cent men. Most of them were in the South, where the average figure was 33 per cent. Significantly, amongst them 'born again' non-whites were more than twice the white proportion: 36 per cent as against 16 per cent. It also found that Evangelicals were on average less educated: 30 per cent had only a grade school education and only 12 per cent went to college (very low for the US). They were mainly in manual and clerical occupations, and in rural rather than urban areas (*New York Times*, 7 September 1980). The majority were therefore blue-collar and minor service workers, many of them poor or unemployed.

More significantly, they were not, as the Evangelical leadership claimed, monolithic in their support of the Republican Party. In 1980 63 per cent voted for Reagan, which meant that 37 per cent voted for Carter (admittedly, also a 'born again' candidate). Reagan's vote rose to 73 per cent in 1984, but that was at the peak of 'the great communicator's' popularity. Meanwhile, black Christians, more 'born again' than the whites, voted nine to one against Reagan in both elections (*New York Times*, 8 November 1984). But less than one fifth of the majority, white and non-white, were self-labelled Evangelicals, which given the low turnout meant that they represented only 11 and 14 per cent of the two successive electorates.

Their leaders still claimed to be influential in Republican counsels and to have swung the election for Reagan, though at that time they did not break the Democratic hold on Congress, or at least the House. Many moderate Republicans feared that they would capture the Party caucuses, especially in crucial areas of the South where dedicated Evangelicals worked hard to win the leadership positions in the local constituencies. In some states like Texas and Tennessee they did influence teaching in the schools, with equal time to 'Creationism' and Darwinian evolution, a ban on sex education, and censorship of 'secular humanist' textbooks, meaning any books which did not support their own views.

Their aim was to impose the Moral Majority's programme on the Party, as set out in Falwell's seven principles: the dignity of human life (anti-abortion); the traditional monogamous family (obedience to the patriarch and no divorce); common decency (no nudity, pornography, gay rights, or sexual licence); the work ethic (enthusiastic labour for workers at minimum wage and no complaints about executive pay); the Abrahamic covenant (Americans as the chosen people, with a special duty to protect the Jews and aid the state of Israel); God-centred education (principally tax-funded school prayer in state schools); and the divinely ordained institutions of home, church, and government (all of course white-male dominated). If all seven were not adopted, according to Falwell 'American would face the judgment of God' (Strege, in Johnson and Tamney, *op. cit.*, p. 122).

Unfortunately for Falwell and the leaders of the Christian Right, they were not even united amongst themselves. One well-informed political commentator, Richard V. Pierard, spoke of 'a cacophony of evangelical voices on Capitol Hill', which cancelled out each other's influence. The chief difference was between those who believed in 'community-building' and 'individualism-preserving' religion; it was the individualists whose ideology chimed with the free-market capitalism of the Republicans who had most influence over the Party[7]. Yet even they were used by the Party rather than using it to enact their own programme. As Pierard pointed out, their claim to help Reagan to the presidency was spurious: he owed more to the failure of Jimmy Carter to cure the massive inflation of the 1970s, and much more to the Iranian hostage crisis which his election team was accused of fostering (the release of the diplomatic hostages immediately after Reagan's election has still not been plausibly explained).

After Reagan's election, the Christian Right did not gain access to the inner sanctum of political power. They soon found he was a more traditional conservative than they had expected. For all practical purposes the New Christian Right found itself disregarded, the media soon began ignoring them, and the 1982 mid-term Congressional elections made it obvious that it did not possess the clout it had claimed to have (Pierard, in Tamney and Johnson, *op. cit.*, pp. 90–92). They came into their own again during the impeachment of Clinton, when they stoked up the hysteria about 'adultery in the White House'. But the failure of their allies—the special prosecuter

Kenneth Starr, a self-styled born-again Christian, and adulterous politicians with second wives like Bob Dole, Jesse Helms, and Newt Gingrich—to make the charges stick undermined their impact still further. The American people voted in the opinion polls against the accusers rather than the sinner: 'Let him that is without sin cast the first stone.'

The fundamentalists were also weakened by their internecine disputes about theology. They were divided about 'the last days', between pre-millennarians who believed that when the 'Rapture' came the true believers would be swept into heaven straight from their cars or beds before Armageddon struck, and post-millennarians who believed that they would have to endure the cataclysm before the sheep were separated from the goats. They were also divided between true fundamentalists who saw the Bible as the undiluted word of God, and the less fundamentalist who accepted there were problems of transcription and translation. Against them both were the Pentecostals and Charismatics like the Toronto Blessing ('slain in the spirit ... ecstasy without the need of drugs') or the Heaven's Gate cult (via the Hale-Bopp comet straight to God) who thought that God's message was *now* (usually through some divinely inspired guru like Jim Jones or David Korresh) which superseded Holy Writ[8].

Their influence on Republican counsels was also weaker in practice than they expected. They had to defend themselves against the charge of attempting to hijack the Party. Falwell was forced to declare in 1981: 'Moral Majority, Inc. is not a religious organisation attempting to control government ... We simply want to influence government, not control government.' In the event Reagan and Bush disappointed the purists. They embraced school prayer and anti-abortion, but did not seriously try to carry them into law; and the swing to the right was opposed by the pragmatic centre who feared the electoral consequences of an Evangelical takeover. Far from capturing the Party, they became, with their emphasis on extreme individualism along with patriarchy and anti-'socialism' (meaning any government intervention or provision of welfare), 'a diffuse ideological justification for US capitalism.'

By 1986 Falwell transformed the Moral Majority into the Liberty Federation, seeking a wider political base amongst religious conservatives. The final denouement came with Pat Robertson's run for the Republican presidential nomination in 1987–88, which turned into a fiasco. They became in effect a mere pressure group on the far right of the Party, their main emphasis, like secular right-wingers, on low taxes, reduced welfare, the nuclear family, condemnation of single mothers, but also of abortion and divorce (both of which policies increased single parentage), the work ethic, and God's blessing on labouring in one's vocation and obeying those in authority, including employers and government. Theirs was an ideal religious policy for a society based on the free-for-all market. But a moral majority in either sense they were not.

Religion as Big Business

All societies need to extract surplus resources from the producers to support collective services like administration, law and order, defence, and so on, and religious institutions belong to that category of service providers. Like other elites, too, religious leaders may be tempted to overdo it and extract a larger share than is strictly necessary for them to carry out their functions, thus provoking discontent and rebellion. The Catholic Church discovered this at the time of the Renaissance, when the grandiose cathedrals, palaces, art works, and high living of clerical princes led inexorably to protest against corruption and church taxation (tithes and indulgences) and thus to the Reformation and loss of universal power.

American churches are much better than European at raising money, and American church-goers are generous, some of them like the Assemblies of God, the Mormons and some Baptist churches voluntarily tithing their incomes. The main Protestant churches raise twice as much per head as the Catholics, three times as much as the Christian Scientists and the Unitarians (*New York Times*, 26 July 1997). The separation of church and state lends itself to religious fund-raising, since almost anyone can set up a church and claim tax exemption.

The traditional churches are left financially in the shade by the new televangelist churches, whose radio and TV programmes devote a disproportionate part of their output to begging for money. They engage in what Lawrence Moore has called 'Selling God'. (Moore, who holds that 'Religion in America is up for sale'—book jacket[9]) Celebrity preachers like Jerry Falwell, Pat Robertson, Jimmy Swaggart, Oral Roberts, Robert Schuller, Henry Lyons, and Jim Bakker make millions of dollars and live in luxury like the CEOs of giant corporations, which in fact they are. Pat Robertson literally talked up an investment of $37,000 borrowed from his parents into his $200 million Christian Broadcasting Network, which he recently sold to Rupert Murdoch. He invested the proceeds in the Bank of Scotland, which was then shamed by its customers and shareholders into giving it back. In compensation the Bank had to pay Robertson £10 million for breaking the contract (*Guardian*, 3 March 1999). This transaction proved that Robertson's main aim was to make money for himself rather than for God.

Oral Roberts, the Pentecostalist, entered 'Blessing Pacts' with his television audience and promised them that, if they sent him $100, they would within a year receive more than the gift back from an unexpected source. When the magic did not work fast enough, he cried abject tears on television that, if they did not send him $8 million dollars within the month, 'the Lord would take him.' The Lord did not, but Roberts received enough donations to continue his lavish life style.

One of the most successful televangelists, before his fall from grace, was the diminutive Pentecostalist Jim Bakker of the PTL (Praise the Lord) Club, who boasted: 'We have a better product than soap or automobiles. We sell eternal life.' He and his heavily painted wife Tammy achieved some 12 million listeners and viewers, an income of $3.7 million a year, palatial homes, a private jet plane, and the Heritage USA theme park that sold more time-share holidays than it could provide. He paid $367,000 to his mistress Jessica Hahn to buy her silence, and his assistants John Ankerberg and John Wesley Fletcher ('I was Jim Bakker's homosexual prostitute') accused him of homosexual practises. After a three-year trial on twenty-four counts of fraud and conspiracy, Bakker was found guilty of embezzling $158 million of PTL members' contributions, and sentenced to 45 years in prison and a half-million dollar fine. It was later reduced to eight years, and he was paroled after five. His wife and partner Tammy Faye, after alcohol detoxification at the Betty Ford Clinic and several adulterous affairs, was hired by Rupert Murdoch's Fox Television for a slightly risqué talk show. Roe Messner, her second husband, was sentenced to 27 months in jail for concealing $400,000 when he and the PTL went bankrupt (*New York Review of Books*, 29 May 1997). But Evangelicals can be born yet again if they publicly repent their sins and are forgiven by their congregation, and Bakker and Jimmy Swaggart, who also was found in the arms of a prostitute, still preach and pray over the airwaves and beg for tax-exempt donations.

Such evidence only emerges during law suits, for obvious reasons, and is in short supply for most religious CEOs, who are not obliged to pay taxes until they are found embezzling church funds. Fraud is not confined to white Evangelists. The Rev. Henry J. Lyons, President of the (mainly African-American) National Baptist Convention, was exposed when his wife set fire to the $700,000 house she found he shared along with a Rolls-Royce with his 'close friend and business partner' Bernice Edwards. Ms. Edwards had already been convicted in 1994 of embezzling $60,000 of federal funds intended for a school in Milwaukee, and Lyons himself had served one year's probation and paid $85,000 restitution for federal bank fraud. Like his penitent brethren, he was forgiven by the congregation, one of whom remarked that 'God didn't say a pastor can't make money' (*New York Times*, 12 July 1997). But Henry has sinned again and has served a custodial sentence.

Most televangelists, no doubt, operate within the law, which despite the constitutional separation of church and state is surprisingly generous to religionists, allowing almost any church or sect to claim exemption from taxation. This seems to cover their lavish living expenses as well as ecclesiastical and charitable purposes. They thus live tax-free, like *ancien regime* aristocrats, at the expense of their flocks. They are in business and reap their rewards in this world as well as in the next. Why do their followers support their luxurious life style and forgive them their trespasses again and again? That brings us to the economic status and psychological character of the fundamentalist multitude.

The Heterogeneous Following

Without a massive oral survey which neither leaders nor followers would welcome, one can only guess at what motivates the fundamentalist flock to donate such large sums to their celebrated preachers. They are not all poor and uneducated citizens of the rural South and the slums of big cities, what Americans call poor white trash and the ghetto blacks. Many are well-heeled, middle-class church-goers of the traditional kind, like those who fill the 2,000 plus seats of Robert Schuller's Crystal Cathedral in California several times over every Sunday. Some are modestly successful business people who need to be assured that making money is not sinful: the parable of the self-multiplying talents is put to constant use here, much more than the camel and the needle's eye. Some are avid consumers who are told that living it up at Bakker's Heritage USA, with its swimming pools and 163-foot waterchute, just like their secular brethren, is part of God's plan for joy on earth. Some, like Madonna, John Travolta, Tom Cruise, Nicole Kidman and Barbra Streisand who support and defend L. Ron Hubbard's Church of Scientology, or Mia Farrow, Jane Fonda and the Beatles who have endorsed the Maharishi Mahesh Yogi of the 93 Rolls-Royces, are multi-millionaire Hollywood celebrities, who find that wealth and fame do not sufficiently satisfy the soul.

Despite this heterogeneity, the great majority of donors to the preachers of the ether, however, are ordinary blue-collar and routine service workers from the lower end of the income range. These are the people who have lost out in the pursuit of the American dream and seek consolation. They, like the preachers, are anti-modernist, anti-intellectual, politically conservative, and eager adherents of the free market. Unlike their leaders, however, they are not winners in the competition for the good things of this world. Being for the most part poorly educated, they do not understand they are being manipulated and exploited. They feel that the system is giving them a bad deal, but they look for remedy in the consolations of religion rather than through political and economic reform. They profoundly believe that their problems stem from high taxes, big government, bureaucracy, welfare scroungers, unwelcome immigrants, and ethnic competitors for jobs and housing. They hate 'socialism', as the Republicans and many Democrats call any attempt to help them with better health care, education, or social security. They are ideal propaganda targets for cynical right-wing politicians who promise them cost-free policies like school prayer and 'pro-life' bans on abortion, and they bless and defend their religious leaders' huge incomes and exemption from taxation. They suffer from a reversal of the Christian message: the poor give voluntarily to the rich and the rich are the first through the needle's eye to heaven. To that extent they are also victims of global capitalism along with the poor of the Third World, though only in relative terms, not absolute material ones.

If this were all, it would be sad, but not perhaps tragic. Unfortunately, the alliance between right-wing fundamentalism and American corporate capitalism comes with a higher price tag. Fundamentalist intolerance for abortion, contraception, women's liberation, gay rights and other 'sins' goes along with support for patriarchy, macho behaviour like the so-called Peace-keepers and Iron Men, and worst of all the peculiarly American gun lobby. This deadly combination leads, unwittingly perhaps, to traditional 'family values', meaning tying wives to kitchen and bedroom and the oppression of women and children within the home, the murder of abortionists and the bombing of clinics, the beating up of homosexuals, a world record prison population and the revival of the chain gang, and a murder rate ten times that of civilised Europe.

American fundamentalism is an intolerant version of Christianity and, while less lethal than its avatars in medieval heretic burners and the early modern witch hunters, its adherents still attempt, in some cases at least, to impose their will by undemocratic and even violent means. Their foundation text is the Old Testament rather than the New, the jealous wrath of Jehovah, not the loving Sermon on the Mount. They preach the tribal hatred of the God of Moses for the Canaanites and blow the ram's horn of destruction against the walls of their Jebusite enemies. Jesus came to replace the old law of 'Thou shalt love thy neighbour and hate thine enemy' with the new Gospel of 'Love your enemy, bless them that curse you, do good to them that hate you' (Matthew, V:43–44). But hate is a more powerful motivation in politics than love, especially in the two-party, first-past-the-post system of the United States. Hence its usefulness to the rich and powerful on the right, who need whatever supernatural help they can get to neutralise the egalitarian threat from the democratic people.

Paradoxically, fundamentalism in the United States both reacts against and embraces globalisation on the corporate capitalist model. While it diverts and exploits the discontents of the victims, its leaders enjoy all the benefits of a materialist, luxurious consumer society. To that extent it confirms in a paradoxical way that fundamentalism is a response, both for and against, to Western globalisation.

Notes

1 Harold Perkin, 'The Tyranny of the Moral Majority: American Religion and Politics since the Pilgrim Fathers' in *Cultural Values*, vol. 3, no. 2, April 1999, pp. 182–95.
2 Lawrence Kaplan, ed., *Fundamentalism in Comparative Perspective*, Amherst, University of Massachusetts Press, 1992.
3 Godfrey Hodgson, *America in our Time*, New York, Vintage, 1976, p. 422.
4 Merle D. Strege in Stephen D. Johnson and Joseph B. Tamney, eds., *The Political Role of Religion in the United States*, Boulder Westview Press, 1986, p. 111.
5 Garry Wills, *Under God: Religion and American Politics*, New York, Simon and Schuster, 1990.
6 Andrew M. Greeley, *Religious Change in America*, Cambridge, Mass, Harvard University Press, 1989.

7 Peter L. Benson and Dorothy L. Williams, *Religion on Capitol Hill*, New York, Harper and Row, 1982.
8 Philip Richter in Stephen Hunt, Malcolm Hamilton and Tony Walter, eds., *Charismatic Christianity*, London, Macmillan, 1997, pp. 97–119.
9 Lawrence D. Moore, *Selling God: American Religion and the Market Place of Culture*, New York, Oxford University Press, 1994.

The Quiet Continent: Religion and Politics in Europe

COLIN CROUCH

COMPARED with the other world regions discussed in this book, contemporary Europe seems religiously to be a very placid place. While large majorities of European populations still profess to basic beliefs in God, participation in public acts of worship has dropped to low levels in most countries.[1] In those where it remains relatively high (mainly Ireland, Italy and Poland), it is nevertheless declining rapidly. Behavioural adherence to church teachings also seems to have experienced a severe collapse; the fact that two of the most Catholic countries in Europe (Italy and Spain) now have lower birth rates than highly secular, post-Lutheran Scandinavia provides an eloquent indicator of this.

With reference to the theme of principal interest to this volume—the relationship between religion and politics—there is a similar story of passivity and decline. From the 1970s onwards, the Catholic Church suffered reversals on public policy issues close to its concerns—divorce, contraception and abortion—in Germany, Italy, Spain and more recently Ireland, sometimes in popular referenda among nominally Catholic populations. Meanwhile mainstream Protestant churches long ago gave up trying to exercise much political muscle. The main political achievements of 20th century European Christianity, the Christian democratic parties, were during the 1990s beset with financial and other moral scandals in Italy, Germany and Belgium. While socialist and other parties often shared these problems, they have struck fundamental blows at Christian democracy's claim to moral status.

European Christianity shows few signs of the fundamentalist enthusiasm affecting Christianity in both the USA and many parts of Latin America, a fact which currently leads American Christianity more closely to resemble Islam or Hinduism than its European sister.[2] It is also notable that European Christian quietude extends to both eastern and western parts of the continent. A widely anticipated revival of religion in Eastern Europe following the fall of communism has failed to materialise. While this might have been expected in Orthodox lands, where national churches had come to terms with the Soviet state in the same way that they had for centuries with previous regimes, it has been more surprising in former Catholic countries. This is particularly so in Poland, virtually the most Catholic country in Europe, where the Church had played a major role in organising opposition to the communist regime through its support of the Solidarnosc movement, and through the work of Karol Woytila, the Polish Pope John Paul II. This inability of the east European Christian churches to take advantage of the collapse of communism

© The Political Quarterly Publishing Co. Ltd. 2000
Published by Blackwell Publishers, 108 Cowley Road, Oxford OX4 1JF, UK and 350 Main Street, Malden, MA 02148, USA

contrasts strongly with the role of Islam in the southern parts of the former Soviet empire.

Viewed globally it is legitimate to talk of the 'exceptionalism' of current European secularism. However, if one takes a closer look matters appear more complex. First, if one limits attention to the industrialised world, and takes account of the similar passivity of religion in Australasia and in Japan (both Shinto and Buddhism), it becomes the USA which is the exception. Outside that country it is superficially still possible to argue that modernisation brings with it secularisation, consistent with 19th century rationalist expectations of the incompatibility between a religious standpoint and that of modern science. The USA might then be explicable in terms of its peculiarity as a society of immigrants. The fact that on virtually any indicator the European country which has become most secular and contrasts most strongly with the USA is England,[3] early to modernise and the case which on so many other issues seems to lie partway between the old continent and America, encourages us in this view.

However, this perspective becomes in turn more questionable if we move still closer. First, most evidence of European secularisation has been very recent. The early stages of industrialisation were associated with waves of religious enthusiasm and revival, notably indeed in 19th century Britain.[4] Even in France, which embarked on a long and dramatic opposition to religion in 1789, it was not until the final third of the 20th century that such things as declining church attendance became strikingly apparent. In general, and with the exception of England, the major decline in European church attendance was a phenomenon of the second half of the 20th century.[5] By that time decline in religious participation could be ranked alongside declines in other publicly oriented activities, such as attendance at sporting events or active participation in political parties. It is not at all clear that the main process at work has been some scientific rejection of religious belief. Consistent with this observation is the fact that decline in actual beliefs seems far less marked than that in practice.

Also relevant here is the important insight of David Martin that it was the clash between church and state rather than that between church and science that was fundamental to the weakening of European Christianity in the context of modernisation.[6] In Catholic lands the rejection by the Church of the autonomy of the secular state in the late 19th century, and particularly in the context of the struggle over the control of mass education, led to the alienation of large parts of the population. The Lutheran state churches in Nordic countries, and in a slightly different way the Church of England, took a very diverse path. They had already accepted the comfortable and official role assigned to them by the state, but at the expense of retaining any popular mobilising power, which latter then became embodied in non-conformist and dissident Protestant sects and denominations. This thesis cannot account for the subsequent and rapid demise of non-conformism, but it does help explain the difference between European and US American experience. Because no church was permitted to become an official church in the young USA, religion was left uncontaminated by either church-state conflict or official quietude. It could work without restraint at creating and sustaining enthusiasm, drawing on the important reservoir of immigrant memory in so doing.

Religions of ethnic minorities typically sustain considerably higher levels of adherence than those of the national majority. This is as true of Christian minorities (such as members of both the various Caribbean churches and of the mainly Irish Catholic church in England) as it is of Moslems, Hindus and others. Jews in the Diaspora are more likely to attend synagogue than those in Israel; British Anglicans in expatriate communities are more likely to attend church than those in England. The rhythm of minority religions is very different from that of majority ones. It is a poignant indicator of the security eventually felt by a minority group within its host society when its religion starts to decline. This role of religion as a signifier for ethnic minorities has been particularly important in the life of American citizens, large numbers of whom can see themselves as some kind of ethnic minority.

In this way we can gradually separate the debate over secularisation from simple stories of a modernisation trajectory, and both understand contrasts between Europe and America and also start to approach the internal dynamics of European religion and its weakening.

Grace Davie has described the state of contemporary European religion in terms of 'believing without belonging';[7] it is not belief in God and Christ which has been challenged, but participation in the formal organisations that represent religious belief. This would seem to be a reasonable conclusion based on the English case, but there are problems in generalising it. In a review of religious belief and practice in Germany, Kecskes and Wolf were not able to find evidence of a difference between disbelief (*Glauben*) and experience (*Erfahrung*); rather, people exhibited to different degrees a 'general religiosity' (*allgemeine Religiosität*).[8] Only level of religious *knowledge* seemed to identify a distinctive group. They found similar evidence from studies in the USA. Gerda Hamberg has perceived a process in Sweden which, in direct contrast with Davie, she calls 'belonging without believing'.[9] Although very few Scandinavians attend church or profess religious beliefs, the great majority of teenagers continue to take the fairly strong and active step of being confirmed into the Lutheran faith; and hardly anybody bothers to seek exemption from the voluntary church taxes. More generally in western Europe rates of christenings, confirmations and funerals remains high; religious weddings have declined in the long run, but in most countries have stabilised and even risen slightly in very recent years. The only exceptions to these patterns are England and, following a very recent and rapid decline, the Netherlands. In Germany, where, as in the Nordic countries there are voluntary church taxes, the vast majority continues to pay them.

Furthermore, European churches have not completely lost their capacity to act as rallying points for political and moral claims, in very diverse ways. Government challenges to the place of church schools in France and Spain during the 1980s led to major protest movements. The collapse of the Christian democratic party in Italy did not lead to the disappearance of Christian democracy, but to its split into three parties, each following a coherent part of the previously very heterogeneous legacy of the movement and thus aligning with left, right and centre. If anything, Catholic social thought has thereby been able to spread its influence more diffusely through Italian political life. Even in the UK during the 1990s public expressions of grief at the untimely deaths of John Smith, then Leader of the Labour Party, and Diana, Princess of Wales, sought for essentially religious forms. In Scandinavia, especially Norway, Protestant Christian movements have shown a surprising new capacity to articulate public discontent over certain directions taken by modernisation, particularly abortion—though this, as well as European Catholic anti-abortion campaigns, take a very different form from the sometimes murderous activities of the anti-abortion movement in the USA.

We can agree with Grace Davie and her colleague Danièle Hervieu-Léger when they argue that contemporary Europeans seem merely to want to know that religion is *there*, that the churches continue to exist, even if they do not want to do very much to guarantee their existence or spend much time inside them.[10] Serious proposals for the abolition of religions would be opposed by very many who were neither members or even believers. There is, as Davie expresses it, a religious 'memory', which 'mutates'.[11] At one extreme this can be little more than an affection for historic buildings and practices providing a link with earlier times; at the other it indicates a concern to have continued access to sources of values not otherwise available within modern society nor created by its massive diversity of institutions and intellectual productions. In particular, people need to come to terms with difficult issues raised by contemporary scientific advance, especially in the medical field. Decisions about the termination of lives of those being artificially sustained by medical apparatus, the ethics of transplant surgery, the use of human genetic material and similar developments are raising moral dilemmas which no secular system of thought—certainly not that of science itself—can really answer. Churches are among the few institutions which have developed anything like expertise on these questions, and their experts are turned to as relevant, even by those who do not necessarily support the conclusions they reach.

The reaching for a religious memory, which is involved in both a minimal 'heritage' approach to religion and a more profound searching for help with timeless and unanswerable ontological questions, relates also to the search for meaning and identity which are always fundamental to religious matters. Pursuing this path then helps us both to explore further the continuing value Europeans place on their religions, and the reasons for the prevailing weakness of those religions.

Identity and Individualism

One of the clearest abiding strengths of religion for modern and even for self-proclaimed post-modern populations is its capacity to confer identity, to help answer the question 'who am I?' In this basic respect, early 21st century men and women differ little from their predecessors throughout human history. In order to make use of the superior intelligence and sensitivities that our species enjoys in relation to those of other animals, we require some sense of meaning. The routine of dust to dust and ashes to ashes, or the idea that we are simply the means by which DNA reproduces itself, seem otherwise to mock and render worthless all that intelligence and sensitivity, our capacity to love and therefore to grieve and to mourn loss. Religions, which relate our lives to a wider cosmos and inform us of a meaning and purpose, have long filled this need. Secular religions, which teach us to relate our lives to the unfolding of a particular history—of an ideology, a nation, a movement, perhaps today of a great corporation—can often achieve the same ends, but religion has repeatedly shown a capacity to outlast these others. It is only for a reflective minority that the great ontological questions appear as a frequent and pressing concern, but from time to time very many people pay some attention to them, and they like to know that there is something with which they can identify which resolves these matters for them, and that there are some specialists out there who devote their care and intellects to looking after it all. At certain moments—typically deaths and disasters—everyone temporarily draws closer to these specialists. For the rest of the time it is enough to know that they are there; and it would be very unsettling if they disappeared.

But identity is not primarily abstract and intellectual. It is mediated through membership of a wider collectivity of those who share it. For day-to-day purposes, the meaning of being, say, a Roman Catholic is not to entertain certain active beliefs in the precise character of the Holy Trinity or transubstantiation. It is to live among other Catholics and to know oneself to be one of that group rather than of another. With the exception of extreme forms of anchorites and hermits, religious life, whether serious and professional or that of marginal acknowledgements, comprises shared membership of a human community of similar others, a membership which in turn relates the individual to some more external source of meaning. Although original Protestantism insisted on the ability and duty of the individual to communicate directly with God, Protestants rapidly formed communities, churches and other groupings. In religious terms their individualism has come to mean largely a capacity for organisational fission and fragmentation of group, not individualistic isolation.

This is what remains of religious faith after all kinds of specific beliefs have been discarded or refuted: a sense of linkage to a profound source of meaning, mediated through membership of a recognised human community of fellow adherents. The precise status of beliefs—about the place of the earth within the universe, the creation of species, or the problematic character of the soul in the context of modern medical capacities artificially to sustain life—do not ultimately matter if identities of this kind are at stake. This explains why Christianity has bounced back after any number of refutations of its specific claims.

If the provision of identity has been a stable aspect of the role of religion over a long historical period, the particular form of that role has changed enormously. It can include making sense of the universe and one's place in it. It can imply an obligation to assist, and a right to claim assistance from, others with the same identity; and a similar obligation to shun or even hate those with a different one. Or, as sometimes today, religious identity can be almost a kind of fashion item: a set of distinguishing characteristics chosen within a market of alternatives in order to be associated with a trend, possibly to be discarded when the fashion changes. In at least this last form identity is very compatible with the contemporary stress on individuality. We assert our personal identity through a series of affirmations of particular characteristics, whether these are a matter or profound beliefs or modes of eating and dress. The particular package we construct forms our individuality, but nearly all the specific components are drawn from identities—even or perhaps especially fashion-oriented ones—shared with others and which normally align the self with those others and indicate a willingness to conform with their ways in order to demonstrate acquisition of the identity. Only very rarely is individualism expressed as complete isolation from a group, and this usually marks out the individual concerned as somewhat strange. Usually individuality is bounded by strong contextual referents. The Greek monks who practise the individualised rituals made possible by the Greek Orthodox Church do so within the recognisable collective frame of Greek Orthodoxy. The extraordinary range of idiosyncrasies practised by Californians are recognisably Californian.

However, by the late 20th century people in the advanced countries seemed more concerned than in certain past periods to construct individual personal packages of such identities. This is not just post-modern theorising about the behaviour of a few exotic cultural elites, but something which sociological research shows us to have been taking place in at least rudimentary form on a very widespread basis. For example, research on the family suggests that young people now have very high expectations of individual fulfilment from relationships and wish to be able to revise decisions and commitments that do not succeed; a low value is placed on commitment to others as opposed to the achievement of the aims of the needs of the individual self—a point which seems to explain the paradox that divorce rates are usually higher among those who postpone marriage until a trial period of cohabitation than among those who make an early commitment to marriage.[12] In such a context, people become very wary about how much heteronomy they are accepting if they adopt an identity in its entirety, and they therefore seek to negotiate their own personal formula within it.

There are difficulties when such a concept of individuality confronts the concept of organisational authority which forms a fundamental part of the community of most forms of European religion. At this point a closer look at contemporary American Christianity provides valuable clues. The large, rather hierarchical forms which are dominant in European Christianity and which are there experiencing decline are also having difficulties in their capacity to attract and retain adherents in the Americas: in the USA Roman Catholicism, Lutheranism, Episcopalianism; in Latin America Catholicism. The ones that thrive in both north and south America are the more loosely structured, constantly fragmenting and re-forming forms of Protestantism.

The apparent capacity for mobilisation embodied in a faith like Catholicism in Italy, where 75 per cent of the population are to be found in church monthly, or Lutheranism in Sweden, securing confirmation in the faith by 80 per cent, is illusory. The compromise between European churches and their populations is that tokens of identity will be retained and even valued, but this comes at the price of the church not being able to insist on any behavioural conformities in return.

The kind of conformity required by the classic organised churches threatens individualism as it came to be understood in the late 20th century. Europeans seem to solve this problem by retaining certain basic links to their faith (such as confession of very rudimentary beliefs, confirmation, payment of a church tax or very occasional participation in Communion), but they are not prepared to get sufficiently close to their church to permit its organisational hierarchies to determine their life choices. In the USA, where there has never been an established church, it is easier to adopt the alternative solution, not so readily available to Europeans with their strongly rooted concepts of what constitutes a church, of choosing from a variety of very loosely structured forms of church and founding new ones at frequent intervals. A further alternative, practised by small but prominent groups of Americans and to a lesser extent Europeans, is to shift to one or other of the non-Christian, non-traditional forms of new age religion. This does not mean that no forms of American new Protestantism or new age religion impose strict requirements on their adherents. Some of them certainly do. However, the particular package of rules has been selected by the individual within a market of alternatives; it is not simply presented as already existing as dominant within the community and prior to the individual's choice as is the case with the standard forms of organised Christianity.

Campiche, using the terminology of Pierre Bourdieu, makes a similar point when he remarks that young Swiss people still want *un habitus religieux*; but they will not accept *une tradition confessionnelle*.[13] Willaime describes how young French people have similarly indicated their desire for an individually defined religion in replies to opinion polls.[14] At its weakest this amounts to religion as an element of life-style, alongside one's taste in music or perhaps only as a fashion statement; Willaime talks of religion *à la carte*. Voyé makes the point with reference to contemporary Belgium—though he could have referred to almost anywhere in contemporary Europe—that while people are willing to adhere to the great rites of the Church, they are no longer willing to *obey it*.[15] Similarly in Italy, home of the Vatican, the Catholic church survives (and in many respects thrives) by accepting considerable diversity in beliefs and religious practice.[16]

Churches have been becoming more tolerant of their members discovering their own form of worship and faith within the framework of previously dogmatic forms. This is seen perhaps most strongly in both Catholic and Protestant churches in the Netherlands and Switzerland. In these religiously plural societies, once Catholic and Protestant hierarchies had begun to take an ecumenical approach towards each other, it was difficult to sustain a rigid insistence on doctrine within any one church; less than a third of Swiss Christians believe that there is any important doctrinal difference between the two principal forms of western Christianity.[17] This is a point to which we shall return.

In addition to these recent changes, which the Catholic Church joined at the time of the Second Vatican Council under Pope John XXIII, some European churches have long embodied this kind of internal diversity: Danish Lutheranism; the diversified localism of Spanish Catholicism; Greek Orthodoxy. Also, in general the major European churches are today less challenged by either internal fragmentation or organised secularism than in the 19th century. Indeed, organised anti-religion has suffered far greater reversals than organised religion, with the collapse of humanist, Marxist and other organisations. This has, however not been enough to protect them from the consequences of individualisation. To explain this, we must search for some further problems of European Christianity, and we can find these by moving closer to the core theme of this volume: the relationship of religion to politics.

The Problematic Politics of European Christianity

In the immediate post-war period Christian democratic parties proved to be the most potent single political force in western Europe, dominating politics in several countries—principally Germany, Italy, Austria, the Netherlands and Belgium—and informing the foundation of the European Economic Community. This dominance had not been anticipated. The Catholic Church itself had expected a continuation of the earlier growth of an aggressively secular liberalism and even more aggressive socialism or communism which had successively dominated political change between the French Revolution and the rise of fascism. Catholic social thinkers were preparing the latest twist to the Thomist doctrine of subsidiarity to protect the rights of Christian localities against what were expected to be inevitably secularist, centralising national governments.

Before the Second World War Christian democrats had been a minority force even within Christian politics, many other elements of which were not at all at ease with the trade unionism, support for welfare spending and redistribution that democratisation implied. In the period between the two world wars most forms of continental European conservatism, Christian or lay, which had not adopted a Christian democratic path had become associated with fascism or nazism, and by 1945 were politically discredited.[18] Not only was Christian democracy the only force capable of displaying proven democratic credentials while contesting both liberalism and socialism, but it became the banner under which all anti-liberals and anti-socialists had to rally, whatever their previous politics. In the process Christian democracy both grew in size and lost much of the radical edge of its policies.[19]

There were other aspects of the legacy of the first half of the 20th century, and of the Cold War which succeeded it for most of the second half, which had further consequences for the character of post-war Christian politics. In the wake of fascism and nazism, animosities and hatreds based on ethnic and other forms of cultural difference, once quite fundamental to many aspects of Christian identities, became completely taboo for all responsible, large-scale religious organisations. Particularly in Germany, this aversion to a politics of hostility and accentuation of differences was compounded by a sense that divisions among Christians, and also between them and other anti-totalitarian forces, had made possible the dominance of nazism in the first place. A repetition must not be risked. An ecumenical spirit among Christians and a hand of friendship to democratic and tolerant non-Christians became *de rigeur*.

A second fundamental condition of the post-war years was the need to avoid a communist future. Liberal and social democratic opponents could no longer be regarded by Christian politicians as anathema, since links with them were needed in a common anti-communist front. They might be organised in different parties, but compromises must be made with their policies, and they must be accepted as potential coalition partners. This was particularly important in France and Italy, where communist parties dominated working-class politics.

These various factors combined to impart a new and initially clear profile to post-war European Christian politics: it had to be ecumenical, accommo-dating, peace-loving—except where communism and any fascist recidivism were involved. It could not allow itself and the identities it conferred to be used to define boundaries of enmity and hatred. In Germany, Catholics and Protestants joined political forces within one party; in the Netherlands and Switzerland they intensified their already existing accommodations with each other. A rapprochement had to be made with, and forgiveness sought from, the surviving remnant of European Jewry. And as new non-Christian immigrants began to arrive from Islamic and other parts of the world during the 1960s, the established churches were careful to avoid any implica-tion in racist movements, but preached toleration and the need to provide a welcome.

Important exceptions can be found to all this; specific groups, including priests, involved themselves in fascist, racist or anti-immigrant movements; and such movements could use an historical Christian rhetoric to defend their stances. Accepted anti-communism could be used as a pretext for fundamentalist opposition to a wider range of politics. As late as the mid-1950s Dutch Catholic bishops threatened excommunication to anyone voting for the Labour Party, moderately social democratic though that party was. But, with the exception of that last, most actions of this kind were minoritarian, secret, and likely to be greeted with repulsion by mainstream church leaders.[20]

Distinctive though this profile of tolerance was, it imparted an ultimately debilitating character to post-war European Christianity. An identity which is reluctant to stress its separateness from others and refuses to stir up latent antipathy towards outsiders is fighting with one hand tied behind its back. Harmless, and therefore rarely hated itself, it could remain as a quiet source of identity; people could be glad that it was still there. But its capacity for militant mobilisation was lost. A Dane might feel that her residual attachment to the national church was an important if placid expression of her Danishness; but she could not then use it to express her resentment at the arrival of Arabs and Turks in the streets of Copenhagen, because church leaders would be stressing tolerance.

On the other hand, in asserting *their* distinctiveness within a host society, the ethnic and religious minorities that are increasingly to be found within European societies have not needed to express hostility and aggression towards the majority, though in some cases they might do so. A perceived need to retain an important indicator of distinctive identity provides an adequate motive, which may extend in its intensity from a fear of extinction of a heritage to a fashion statement. For a majority culture or ethnicity to respond in a similar way appears, however, aggressive.

Two contrasting examples express all these points particularly well. Both the Netherlands and Northern Ireland contain large Catholic and Protestant (mainly Calvinist) populations; both societies have organised virtually their entire public life around this division for a considerable time. To know the religion of a Dutchman or Ulsterman was also to know which newspapers he would read, to which voluntary organisations he would belong, in which streets he was likely to live, which sports teams he was likely to support, and of course for which parties he would vote. In the Netherlands this framework of separation, once a source of considerable inter-community antagonism, was pacified by being formally recognised and incorporated into a system of cross-faith co-operation. This was in turn gradually affected by the post-war European context of rapprochement. Little or nothing was done to stress separateness and difference; opportunities for co-operation were always seized. While the organisational forms embodying the different communities have survived, they have lost meaning and purpose in everyday life. From being one of the countries with the highest levels of religious service attendance in Europe, the Netherlands changed rapidly from the late 1960s onwards to rival England in its absence of religious observance.

Northern Ireland was entirely exempted from the general post-war trends in religion and politics described above by the fact that the dispute over the political status of the territory kept alive the Reformation conflict and, more specifically, the armed conflict on Irish soil in the 1680s between Catholic and Protestant claimants to the English throne as more salient events than the confrontations with fascism and communism on which minds were concentrated elsewhere in Europe. Catholics and Protestants alike continued to use their religion as a means of identifying themselves and their heritage as separate from and hostile to the other community. Religious adherence here remained until the end of the 20th century at a considerably higher level than in the rest of the United Kingdom.

In its almost universal refusal to assert itself aggressively and negatively against outsiders, European Christianity resembles or is indeed part of the wider question of the problem of a European political identity. If official enthusiasts for European integration accepted no self-imposed limitations on their attempts to encourage European populations to identify themselves as Europeans, they would stress the racial and religious distinctiveness of a white, western, Catholic/Protestant people, threatened (by low birth rates and constant immigration pressure) with demographic and cultural invasion by Orthodox Slavs from the east and Arab and North African Muslims from the south, all seeking to rob west Europeans of their hard-won prosperity. Add a blatant anti-Americanism towards an alien force to the west, and there might be powerful ethnic appeal that could span the left-right spectrum. This could be considerably more potent in forging a European identity than the current practice of financing a few road schemes and culture festivals.

Neither the European Commission nor the churches will do anything of the kind. For at least the older members of European political and religious elites memories of the absolute horror produced when a generation in some European countries embarked on a similar enterprise remain strong. The number of members of European political and religious elites willing to break rank and overtly exploit the potential reservoir of aggressive identities to be found here remains small and limited to a fringe, shunned by 'respectable' colleagues. The fact that the issues involved are latently alive and very sensitive only reinforces determination not to follow a path involving any kind of such risks. Eastward extension of membership of the EU will be a cautious matter, particularly as it extends to Islamic Turkey, an issue to which the large Moslem minorities within many EU countries are relevant. It is significant, both that the waiting list for membership of all these countries has been established, and that it takes a particular order: first Catholic and Protestant countries: Poland, the Czech Republic, Hungary and the Baltic states; then some Orthodox Slav lands; then Turkey.[21]

European patriotism has to be of the intellectual Habermasian kind: a love of the humane and liberal qualities of the constitution; certainly not an atavistic passion for the fatherland.[22] Such a phenomenon considerably lacks mobilising power and will never excite the passions. On the other hand, it is highly unlikely to lead to the torture or murder of anyone, and is not without a certain quiet reality in public consciousness. Very much the same is true of European Christianity.

Matters could, of course, change, as memories of the first half of the 20th century fade. Already much of the ecumenical, kindly face of contemporary churches seems to have become a bureaucratised process with little meaning for its professional practitioners; sometimes they seem to be just doing a job, speaking their ecumenical lines just as any corporate executive speaks the lines of the firm currently employing him.[23] This facade could eventually crack in the face of a true fundamentalist revivalism, though there are today no signs that this is imminent. The very non-bureaucratic, charismatic, crusading and in many respects reactionary revivalism of Pope John Paul II has been utterly committed to reconciliation and friendly dialogue with other Christians, with Jews, Muslims and others, extending to direct contact with Fidel Castro. True, Opus Dei, the secretive movement which grew alongside the Franco dictatorship in Spain and has been involved in various non-democratic situations, remains at the heart of the Vatican, but it works quietly and never engages in any anti-democratic or anti-ecumenical mobilisations.

Meanwhile, the specifically political activity of European Christianity is just possibly embarking on its third major reorientation since the start of the democratic era. The first reorientation, in the late 19th century, involved coming to terms with the secular liberal state—a process which took Catholics and Protestants in very different directions. The second, complete by the mid-20th century, involved becoming a rallying point for conservative and capitalist but democratic forces against socialism. The third, if it develops, would align Christians and their former socialist antagonists against neo-liberalism. There are some indications of this. The Lutheran churches of northern Europe have for some time maintained a social gospel; the Church of England long ago left its role of being 'the Tory Party at prayer', and has taken up a number of essentially left-of-centre political positions on issues of the day. The generally conservative papacy of John Paul II has been notable for its defence of the welfare state and of labour rights.[24]

It is important to understand what might be going on here accurately. It is not that the churches 'have become social democrats'. The proper role of churches is to assist mankind to approach God and to tend to the interests of their own organisations. From time to time, however, this fundamental mission leads them to follow empirically parallel paths to various forms of secular politics, leading to varied de facto alliances. At present the European religious and the social democratic agenda coincide in that both have, in their slightly different ways, been bruised by the abrasive form of contemporary interpretations of individualism embodied in neo-liberalism, the current ruling ideology of most of the advanced world.

Neo-liberalism can, however, claim its own alliance with religion. The relatively pure neo-liberalism of the British and US right seems to make increased space for the charitable work of churches and other voluntary organisations in its reduction of the role of the welfare state, which classic social democrats often seemed to want to have a monopoly in this sphere. Further, the conservative stance of most neo-liberals on non-economic issues also chimes with many religious preferences. Similarly, the social democratic form of neo-liberalism, the so-called 'third way', stresses its elective affinity with the 'third arm', the voluntary sector, in welfare, and erects a form of communitarianism in the non-economic sphere to balance the individualism it advocates within the economy. However, in both cases the dominance of the joint stock company maximising shareholder value and deregulating all forms of protection against its power seems to have hollowed out the ostensible pluralism of these forms of neo-liberalism. Concepts such as the stakeholder economy, economic mutualism of the type embodied by British building societies, and similar phenomena which might occupy the space between the state and shareholder capitalism have been squeezed to the margin, as neo-liberalism neither knows how to nor wants to prevent the latter from occupying the whole of the space.

This development seems to be a more salient problem in European societies, including the UK, than in the USA, where there is far less social and ethical criticism of shareholder domination, and where religious groups themselves increasingly use the form of the joint stock company to build their own organisations. Thus European Christians and social democrats seem to stand together in an only partially mutually recognised alliance of those standing for values and practices which are being pushed aside during the current interpretation of the unavoidable logic of modernisation. Even if such an alliance were to become more explicit, giving European religions a renewed focus, it would remain an alliance of the quiet forces, of those bruised by the brusqueness of change and power, apart from the centres of vigorous energy.

Notes

1 C. Crouch, *Social Change in Western Europe*, ch. 9, Oxford, Oxford University Press, 1999; European Values Group, *The European Values Study 1981–1990: Summary Report*, Aberdeen: Gordon Cook Foundation, 1992.

2 The US case is well discussed elsewhere in this book. For the Latin American situation, see D. Martin, *Tongues of Fire: The Explosion of Protestantism in Latin America*, Oxford, Blackwell, 1990.

3 The internal diversity of the constituent nations of the United Kingdom is nowhere more apparent than in the field of religion. England here therefore means England, and neither Britain nor the UK as a whole.

4 See several chapters in S. Bruce ed., *Religion and Modernization: Sociologists and Historians Debate the Secularization Thesis*, Oxford, Clarendon Press, 1992.

5 Crouch, *op. cit.*

6 D. Martin, *A General Theory of Secularisation*, Oxford, Blackwell, 1978.

7 G. Davie, 'Contrastes dans l'héritage religieux en Europe', in G. Davie and

D. Hervieu-Léger, *Identités religieuses en Europe*, Paris, La Découverte, 1994; G. Davie, *Religion in Europe*, Oxford, Oxford University Press, 2000.

8 R. Kecskes and C. Wolf, 'Christliche Religiosität: Konzepte, Indikatoren, Messinstrumente', *Kölner Zeitschrift für Soziologie und Sozialpsycholgie*, 45, 2, 270–87, 1993.

9 G. Hamberg, *Studes in the Prevalence of Religious Beliefs and Religious Practives in Contemporary Sweden*, Uppsala, S. Academiae Ubsaliensis, 1990.

10 Davie, *op. cit.* (1994 and 2000); and Hervieu-Léger, D. 'La religion des européens: Modernité, religion, sécularisation', in Davie and Hervieu-Léger, *op cit.*

11 Davie, *op. cit.*, 2000.

12 Crouch, *op. cit.*, ch. 7; R. Lesthaeghe, 'The Second Demographic Transition in Western Countries: An Interpretation', in K. O. Mason and A.-M. Jensen, eds. *Gender and Family Change in Industrialized Societies*, Oxford: Clarendon Press, 1995; R. Lesthaeghe and G. Moors, 'Living Arrangements, Socio-Economic Position, and Values among Young Adults: A Pattern Description for France, West Germany, Belgium, and the Netherlands, 1990', in D. Coleman, ed. *Europe's Population in the 1990s*, Oxford: Oxford University Press, 1996.

13 R. J. Campiche, 'Dilution ou recomposition? Confession en Suisse', in Davie and Hervieu-Léger, *op. cit.*

14 J.-P. Willaime, Laïcité et religion en France', in Davie and Hervieu-Léger, *op. cit.*

15 L. Voyé, 'Belgique: Crise de la civilisation parossiale et recomposition de la croire', in Davie and Hervieu-Léger, *op. cit.*

16 R. Cipriani, 'Diffused Religion and New Values in Italy', in J. A. Beckford and T. Luckmann, eds., *The Changing Face of Religion*, London, Sage, 1989; E. Pace, 'Désenchantement religieux en Italie', in Davie and Hervieu-Léger, *op. cit.*

17 Campiche, *op cit.*, p. 104.

18 Nazis were of course not Christian. Fascists often were, especially in the more conservative forms that dominated in Portugal, Spain and, very briefly, in pre-nazi Austria.

19 For a good study of the social politics of Christian democracy, see K. van Kersbergen, *Social Capitalism: A study of Christian democracy and the welfare state*, London, Routledge, 1995.

20 This was not the case in Portugal and Spain, where the Catholic church hierarchy did very little to stand in the way of the dictatorships.

21 The early admission of Orthodox Greece, and the early position in the queue of Cyprus, are not really exceptions. Greece as *classical* Greece has always been granted a kind of honorary membership of western Christendom.

22 J. Habermas, *Die postnationale Konstellation: politische Essays*, Frankfurt am Main, Suhrkamp, 1998.

23 For an interesting example, see the image of the Church of England revealed in Humphrey Carpenter's biography of the former Archbishop of Canterbury, Robert Runcie, *The Reluctant Archbishop*, London, Hodder & Stoughton, 1996.

24 See the publications of the Pontifical Academy of Social Sciences, Vatican City.

J. N. Figgis, Churches and the State

PAUL HIRST

IN much of the developed West activist organised religion and the liberal state have become increasingly uneasy bedfellows. This is in part because of increasing religious pluralism. To the variety of Christian denominations must now be added a plethora of new cults, but, more significantly, substantial Muslim and other non-European religious communities. The new groups find the existing political settlements between religion and the state problematic. In apparently secular France, Muslims find such practices as forbidding their girls to wear headscarves to state schools symbolic of a situation that is generally discriminatory and unfair. In England Muslims have campaigned against the anomaly that the schools of Christian churches should receive public funds and they should not.

The new conflicts between religious groups and the state have also occurred because of the growth in the number of extremist cults and religious political activism. The most extreme think nothing of using terrorism, such as the Aum Shinrikyo sect in Japan releasing Sarin gas on the Tokyo subway, or fundamentalist Christians in the USA firebombing abortion clinics and shooting doctors. In the USA a new fundamentalist and rightist Christian activism is determined to breach the limits of secularism and to impose its will on the mainstream through law. Thus they organise to pack local schoolboards and Republican primary elections in order to press religious minority agendas on the public as a whole.

In fact, the liberal foundations of the existing settlements between religious groups and the state have many critics, not all of them religious. Those critics often misunderstand the present state of liberal secularism, endowing it with substantive commitments it need not possess. Embattled defenders of liberalism often thicken the doctrine to the point where it becomes prescriptive and exclusive rather than neutral and procedural.[1] Radical advocates of multicultural politics, religious conservatives and many secular liberals all express strong dissatisfactions with the existing state of affairs.

Advocates of multiculturalism, seeking equality of regard for hitherto marginalised groups, frequently see liberalism as a prescriptive 'Western' doctrine, rather than as a recipe for limited government and moral neutrality outside the criminal law. Human rights are seen as inextricably culture-based and when the attempt is made to apply them internationally to other cultures' beliefs and practices, then the effect is to deny the specific identity and validity of those cultures. Within Western societies multiculturalist critics also see liberalism as prescribing substantive values under the guide of neutralism and liberty, such as unconditional freedom of expression. Hence the attempts to impose ever stricter politically correct limits on what counts as derogatory

Published by Blackwell Publishers, 108 Cowley Road, Oxford OX4 1JF, UK and 350 Main Street, Malden, MA 02148, USA

speech. Echoes of this position are to be found in liberal Anglicans' responses to the Rushdie affair. Some clerics saw Muslim anger not as intolerance, but as a sign that deep beliefs had been offended, some going as far as to argue that the offence of blasphemy be rescued from virtual desuetude and extended to cover faiths other than the Christian. Moral and cultural relativism can thus act against political liberalism, arguing that extensive limits on speech and behaviour are needed in order to protect cultural plurality.

Christian conservatives naturally see things rather differently. They regard secularism and the moral neutralism of the liberal state as a fundamental threat to the social order. Liberalism allows people to go their own way, to engage in acts that, while socially destructive, are outside the scope of the criminal law. People may divorce easily, practise adultery and neglect to instill the right values in their children without moral censure or sanction by the state. Thus the Christian right has sought to pursue the reception of its own religious beliefs in the form of 'family values' and to reinforce them through law and public policy.

Defenders of secular liberalism fear such religious political activism and have difficulty in countering it, except by advocating a version of liberalism that is itself strongly committed to a substantive set of social values. The problem for committed liberals is that they cannot prevent the advocacy of illiberal beliefs and policies that stops short of a direct threat of violence and of public disorder. Religious conservatives are thus free to use liberal freedoms to campaign for compulsion in belief. This is an old problem, but more difficult for liberals is the ability of the religious right to turn liberal arguments to their own advantage against secularism and moral neutrality. Thus they argue that the are merely seeking an 'equal chance' for their own beliefs and policies. This has been one of the main methods of advocating the teaching of creationism in public schools in the USA. Evolutionism and creationism are presented as beliefs that are essentially at par and thus both should have equal time in the science curriculum. To deny this is held by fundamentalists to reveal the inherent authoritarianism of modem science, its illiberalism. To claim that evolutionary biology is real science and creationism so much mumbo jumbo is thus to be doctrinaire and to deny others the legitimate right to propagate their beliefs to their children in their schools. When, as in Kansas, religious activists go beyond the doctrine of the equal chance, they switch justifications from freedom of opinion to democracy, defending their policy as giving expression to the will of the people.

The mainstream secular liberal settlement thus seems to satisfy few of those most actively concerned with the relationship between religion and the state. It offends such very different groups as multicultural radicals and religious conservatives. Moreover, it is seen to be dangerously hollow by many liberals themselves. The problem with these very different views is that they share a paradoxically at once inflated and yet impoverished account of why states are secular and, therefore, at least minimally liberal in matters of belief. The critics see this neutralism as the product of liberalism as a positive political doctrine put into practice. Secularism is seen as the product of an activist and doctrinaire liberalism, rather than as an almost inevitable consequence of the situation of religion in modern society and the modern state. Liberalism is at bottom prudential. States have to be limited governments in matters of belief, because the costs of any other policy are insupportable. It is the irreducible plurality of competing religious groups and the diversity of their beliefs that pushes the state toward neutrality.

If religion were to return to its status in Europe at the beginning of the seventeenth century, as the dominant human concern and one to be pursued at the expense of others' belief, then we should be confronted with a situation in which each religious group sought to prevail and to impose its doctrine upon all as the only true belief. The exhaustion of the religious civil wars forced the moderation of this theocratic will-to-power. Religious groups had to accept the *de facto* existence of others and, therefore, limit their own claims to universal domination. Some institutions such as the Papacy failed to accept this and in consequence weakened their political role in relation to the Catholic states in Germany. In Germany religious coexistence was accomplished by religious territorialisation after the peace of Westphalia in 1648. States were established as either Catholic or Reformed. In doing so those states had to accept by terms of the treaties the existence of other states with different religions and to abstain from interfering in their internal affairs. Thus were established the basic principles of the modern concept of sovereignty in its international aspect, mutual recognition and non-interference. From the very beginning, however, sovereignty was limited by the first internationally recognised human right, secured by treaty, that is, to permit the freedom of dissenters from the established state religion to emigrate.[2] In England and Holland the containment of religious conflict was finally achieved, after the bloody struggles of the Eighty Years War and the Civil War, by the toleration of religious communities other than the established church, at the price of the members of such communities being subject to certain restrictions on religious practice and civil disabilities.[3]

Religion is no longer the all-inclusive human concern. Most of even the active religious accept it as a specific practice, and conform to the customs and values current in economic and social life. Moreover, the vast majority of churches and their members now accept the legitimate existence of other religions within the same policy, seeking for themselves only the common rights to propagate doctrine and seek converts. States are secular today because all religions are now sects, they command only the support of their own faithful and the latter are a minority of the religious, let alone the general population. Indeed, in the most actively and untypically religious of the developed countries, the USA, this very fact of continuing mass religiosity promotes religious diversity, as people are converted and choose new religions all the time. A plurality of religious groups in a sovereign territorial state requires, either, that the state be secular, in the sense of being neutral between the sects, and that it practise limited government in matters of belief;

or, that the state adopt the right to persecute on behalf of one religious group whose members have control of political power.

This may seem to put the choice starkly, but few political systems can now support the compromise of an established religion with publicly supported privileges, and a bare freedom to practise their beliefs for others. The position of the Church of England has become laughable in this regard, and in Israel the secular chafe against the interference in social life of the religious authorities. The Lutheran Church has recently been disestablished in Sweden. The difficulty that religious groups face with the state today is not because the state is too neutral, too limited a government, as many of the religious perceive it, but because it is so structured as to be not limited enough. The problem is less that groups (even relatively extreme ones) seek to abolish others and establish a theocracy, as that they are competing to control state legislation and social policy and thus to have their views on how social life should be organised prevail. That means that they are competing directly in religious terms for members and indirectly through the political system in terms of regulating conduct. It is impossible to give the claims of competing groups equal treatment in a sovereign territorial state except by depoliticising and, therefore, neutralising the practice in question, putting it beyond the scope of direct government intervention. Even this will not please all. Otherwise sovereignty and territoriality mean that only one law can prevail. Most states may be secular in the sense of being neutral between the religious claims of the sects, but they are not neutral in other areas over which the religious compete to shape law. Liberal states may be limited governments, but that is because they have chosen to practise self-limitation in certain domains. Formally avowedly secular and liberal states claim both unlimited legislative sovereignty and omnicompetence.

Liberalism and Legal Sovereignty

Such unlimited legal sovereignty has never sat easily with liberalism. This is most obvious in states that based their new representative governments on monarchical foundations, providing new legitimacy for absolutist claims to supreme power. In France the Constitution of 1791 gave the state unlimited legislative sovereignty derived from the will of the people and sought to reconcile this with the limitations on state power implied in the 'rights of man'. In England the revolution of 1688 and the constitutional settlement of 1689 had created an equally unstable combination of the unlimited sovereignty of the Crown-in-Parliament with a Bill of Rights and a commitment to 'the rule of law'. Liberalism—limited government and neutrality in the private affairs of civil society—could only be secured in these circumstances if the absolutist potential of the claim to legislative sovereignty was either not used or not needed. In the former case, it was hobbled by self-imposed constitutional restrictions, and, in the latter case, because the societies in question were sufficiently homogeneous in beliefs and manners that the frontiers of limited government were never really tested.

In fact neither of these routes to containing sovereignty has proved wholly effective. Even in the USA, with its strong, formal limitations on state power in the shape of federalism, the separation of powers and the constitutional guarantee of political rights, the power of the majority in situations of political panic has led to such fundamentally illiberal measures as the Smith Act or HUAC. In most Western societies homogeneity of beliefs and values had only a brief nineteenth century 'bourgeois honeymoon' between the religious conflicts and orthodoxies of early centuries and the social struggles of the twentieth. The effect of the latter conflicts was to destroy liberal government in all but a handful of countries, creating authoritarian conservative, communist and fascist regimes.

In late twentieth century society struggles over social *mores*—over issues like drugs, abortion, gay rights, etc.—have become salient as the scope and influence of compulsory collectivities has declined. Individuals are increasingly free to choose how to live, and they frequently choose to live in ways that escape the old collective disciplines. Major conflicts between the states of the developed countries have ceased, reducing the centrality of national solidarity and the forms of homogeneity in behaviour it legitimated and enforced. Class conflicts and collective labour struggles have diminished too, reducing the claims to conformity of class solidarity. Religious groups are doubly implicated in the new politics of *mores* or, to use a more modern locution, 'lifestyle issues'. On the one hand, they tend to take issue against many of the new sexual and cultural freedoms. On the other hand, they are among the beneficiaries of the new freedom of choice and identification for individuals. It is the evangelical churches and the new age cults that have been most able to attract new converts, growing at a time when most traditional churches have been stagnating or declining. It is these groups that are most politically active of the religious, fuelled by the zeal of new converts. This is true whether it be the New Right in the USA or the role of New Age beliefs in parts of the environmental protest movement. Such religious groups are driven by individuals' choices to convert, not by traditional loyalties. This means that they must continually strive for new converts and to keep existing ones, and this explains at least part of their often strident and noisy political activism.

The current conflicts and dissatisfactions that centre on religion and social *mores* are nothing like the great social conflicts of the century just past, nor the great religious struggles of the Reformation period. This does not mean that they are easy to deal with. Social and political pluralism, the competition of beliefs and social standards, is combined with the attempt by the more activist groups to have their views on the key social issues made into law. The more traditionally religious are horrified by the notion of gay marriages, while liberals and feminists are equally appalled by the Christian right's attempts legally to curtail abortion. These struggles are intractable, because the diversity of views is unlikely to decline and because, as things stand, there can only be one community standard in state law. If the present state of affairs persists, we can expect increasing and ongoing political and social turbulence. This will come not only from the religious but also from other groups seeking to alter and to control *mores*, like the animal rights movement or the more extreme environmental groups. None of these groups, religious or otherwise, can hope to dominate the political system: they do not have enough support, nor do they create enough political energy outside of the specific issue on which they can inspire often fanatical devotion in their followers. If such conflicts are not contained then we can expect ongoing low-intensity 'social wars' that fray the edges of existing liberal settlements even further. How might such competition for community standards be contained and the conflict of competing lifestyle groups mitigated?

The thinker who most clearly linked an understanding of the threat posed by the claim to unlimited sovereignty on the part of the modern state and the need for a new relationship between religious groups and public authority was John Neville Figgis.[4] Figgis was an Anglican clergyman, whose works were mostly written in the teens of the twentieth century. He combined radicalism in thinking about politics with an Anglo Catholic theological stance and a conservative approach to religious values. He advocated a pluralist state, in which greater power would be devolved to associations in civil society. He was also sympathetic to the claims of labour and critical of the greed of the new plutocracy. Yet he was strongly opposed to the liberal dilution of Church doctrine to make it more acceptable to conventional opinion and opposed to accommodation with prevailing social *mores*, for example, being strongly opposed to the Church tolerating divorce. Figgis' understanding of contemporary political problems was reinforced by a deep historical perspective stretching back beyond the rise of the modern state and by his work as an historian of political theory.[5] Figgis was strongly influenced by the great English constitutional and legal historian Frederich William Maitland and by their joint reading of the German historian of the law of associations, Otto von Gierke.

We will concentrate here on three main issues that arise from Figgis' work: his critique of sovereignty; his account of the relationship of churches to the state; and his belief that Christianity was a religion based on freedom and opposed to any spiritual aristocracy. This latter point is central to his perception of the totalitarian potential of the modern state. He anticipated the disasters of communist and fascist regimes, reading the potential for arbitrary power in such phenomena as French anticlericalism and in the rightist reception in Germany of doctrines like Nietzsche's will-to-power and the *übermensch*. The discussion will be drawn from three works: *Churches in the Modern State* (1913), *The Fellowship of the Mystery* (1914) and *The Will to Freedom* (1917).[6]

Paul Hirst

The Problem of Sovereignty

Figgis recognised that modern state sovereignty was a relatively recent phenomenon, that it only began to be shaped in policy and defined in concepts at the end of the sixteenth century. In the Middle Ages authority was fundamentally pluralist in nature, there being neither a single all-powerful ruling body, the state, nor a civil society separate from it and upon which it acted. Various political bodies—monarchs, barons, cities, merchant leagues, guilds, the Church, religious houses—governed and competed with one another in complex and overlapping ways, making claims on the same territory. Territorial authority was strictly subsidiary to the notion of the governance of activities within a single overarching Christian Commonwealth that was greater than and encompassed both the Church and the various rulers. Claims to supreme authority by both Pope and Emperor were disputed by their rival and by other political bodies, like the Italian city-states (who played one off against the other). Early modern political thinkers took the claims to unlimited power and legislative sovereignty that could be traced back to the Roman emperors and applied them to the new institutions of territorially-demarcated centralising states. Modern ruler sovereignty in the institution of the state made real the hitherto largely abstract claims of Roman Imperium. The new monarchies were mostly successful in abrogating local powers and extinguishing particular liberties, centralising the rights to make and administer law, to raise armed forces, to tax, to coin money, and to make treaties.

Modern states inherited this early-modern concentration of power and exclusive government within a definite territory, and they now possessed the fiscal and administrative means to give full effect to it. Even if founded on liberal principles, like the French Third Republic, the modern state claimed an unlimited right to legislate for and over society. The state as sovereign alone had the right to grant powers to act and to order governance, to assign powers to all lesser authorities and to determine the rights of every association. Representative democratic government strengthened the state's hand, since it provided the powerful legitimation of electoral success for action in respect of particular bodies in civil society. The late nineteenth century and early twentieth century was a period in which the concessionist theory of associations held particularly strong sway. This held that all bodies, other than the state itself, existed at the legislature's fiat. The powers that associations enjoyed were revocable concessions of to act by the state. Only the state and the individual were inherently legitimate political actors: the latter as the bearer of rights and as the foundation of legitimacy for the state, and the former as the expression of the will of the people. All other bodies were legal constructs, given their corporate status by the state.

Figgis saw that this concessionist doctrine, if fully applied, pulverised and de-politicised civil society. It destroyed the capacity for genuine self-government and for independent evolution of associations. He was less concerned

110

with the specific features of property law of the exact legal status of corporate personality than to assert that certain associations are properly political too and not just the state. Such associations needed a wider right of self-government. He saw Bismarck's *Kulturkampf* against the Catholic Church in Germany, the anticlerical policies of Emile Combes and the French Radicals, and the concessionist attitudes displayed by lawyers and judges in the Free Church of Scotland case in Britain as examples of the excessive power of the state over religious associations.

Figgis attacked concessionism in terms of the doctrine of the real personality of groups. This he derived principally from Gierke. He used this notion to defend the right to corporate existence and to group self-government in a broader more 'political' sense than that allowed by contemporary political thinking with its exclusive stress on the rights of the state and the individual. He was not interested in the metaphysical idea of the group as an entity distinct from the individuals that make it up, although Gierke had toyed with this in a confused way.[7] Groups existed for Figgis, because individuals were not only socialised into them, but made social by them. Individuals carried the group on in their beliefs and practices, but they were changed and enhanced as individuals by the experience of being members of it. Figgis had no time either for the metaphysical idea of the state as in the British idealists, or for the negative stand-alone individualism of Herbert Spencer. He believed in fellowship rather than in group personality *per se.*

His point was that bodies, like the Catholic Church, were not created by the state. In that case it pre-existed the modern state, and in other cases it arose from a human ability to associate together that did not need state licence to bring new bodies into being. The state could not dictate every aspect of the life of groups without undermining individual freedom and human creativity. Individuals gathered together create social life in associations, and those associations must be free to develop if people are to achieve their common purposes. Figgis claimed, 'this false conception of the State as the only true political entity apart from the individual is at variance not only with ecclesiastical liberty, but with the freedom of all other communal life, and ultimately that of the individual' (Figgis 1913 p. 100).

The concept of sovereignty inherited from early-modern absolutism was sociological nonsense in modern society. It made some sense in the context of appropriating power from the institutions of late-medieval society. Today the state cannot be an absolute sovereign, confronted as it is by a complex organised civil society. The state must recognise the inherently limited nature of its government and it must share power, as in a federation, with the governments in civil society. It must accept the ongoing existence and capacity for development of associations, they too are 'political' bodies. The problem with the claims to sovereignty of the modern state is the coupling of legislative primacy with a highly centralised and powerful administration. Democracy makes the power of the state especially dangerous, it enables rulers to claim that their policy is actually derived from the will of the people and, therefore, in the general interest. Associations thus have no inherent rights, no particular liberties. Liberal states claim to respect the rights of the individual, yet they undermine them when acting against the institutions whereby individuals pursue their common life, such as churches or trade unions. Actually attempting to use the absolutist concept of sovereignty in modern society could only lead to totalitarianism, to the undermining of limited government and to the state control of associations.

Figgis was perceptive to see that modern state sovereignty contained within it the threat of totalitarian power and to see that that threat would be especially directed against religious liberty, for churches make powerful claims on the loyalty of their members that can run counter to those of the state. This danger he saw in the French anticlerical policy to strip the Catholic Church of its property, place that property in the hands of lay bodies, and in effect substantially reduce its capacity for corporate self-government. What did Figgis see as an alternative? He was no anarchist and he did not deny to the public power a *specific* form of primacy over groups. In this respect he was far clearer than later pluralist writers like G. D. H. Cole and H. J. Laski, who in their less cautious moments treated the state as if it were merely just another association. For him, state law must have primacy if groups were to enjoy their own freedoms, otherwise they could threaten each other's rights. Figgis was explicit that associations and churches should govern only their own members and that only with the members' consent: 'what we claim is freedom within the limits of civil society, and that we neither claim to be outside the law nor to exercise control over politics' (Figgis 1913 p. 105).

Figgis envisaged the modern state's proper role as the association of associations. The public power would be a limited rather than an omnicompetent body. It would make the rules to regulate individuals' and associations' conduct. It would secure the freedom of individuals in respect of associations and the rights of associations with respect to one another. Beyond that, it would let associations manage their own affairs and impose their own rules. For example, the state would not prescribe or proscribe books, but it would permit the Catholic Church to do so for its own members and to excommunicate them if they broke the rule. Figgis would thus pick apart legal primacy and governmental omnicompetence. The laws would be supreme but government limited. The state would become the primary source of binding rules in this pluralist political system but one governing body among many. It would have primacy in its specific function, to ensure the stable working of associational governance, but not beyond it.

The state should be secular and to offer through civil law a secular existence to those who wanted it. Religious groups could construct their own moral order and impose it on their own adherents as a condition of membership. That right would be strictly limited to the members who have freely chosen to join the community. Churches and other associations would have to accept a pluralism of beliefs and morals as a condition of their own freedom of self-government, that they are partial institutions within a community of other associations. The cardinal principle of associationalism is thus this mutual recognition of the right to govern in private, to have a polity within one's association, and to respect the wider civil concomitants of that right. For Figgis, the fundamental liberal principle is that, 'We cannot claim liberty for ourselves, while at the same time denying it to others' (Figgis 1913 p. 112). Yet this is exactly what the most fanatical of the politically religious would do today, using the freedoms of political institutions to promote their own cause. The question is whether a pluralist state would maximise opposition to such practices and minimise the stakes of competing for political power? The concentration of political power gives greater scope to those who are able to appropriate it. Power divided and limited reduces the damage that evil people can do if they acquire it and also their incentive to do so. This argument should have a special appeal for Christians, given their belief in the potential of all human beings to sin.

Churches and the State

'The cardinal fact which faces us today is the religious heterogeneity of the modern state' (Figgis 1913 p. 113). Churches are partial institutions within a wider society. Figgis is clear that 'unless you definitely enforce religious belief, the Christian Church, however broadly defined, can only be a sect, a part of the modern nation' (Figgis 1913 p. 132).

This is he says, 'the result of the principle of toleration' (*ibid.*). Sociologically religious pluralism and, therefore, toleration is inescapable, as Figgis saw; but what of the religious who deny it? Clearly the classical liberal arguments will have little force. The prudential arguments for toleration need some reinforcement against those who would persecute in the interests of faith. How to challenge the idea of enforced belief? The answer ultimately can only be presented in religious terms to those who think in a religious idiom. This, of course, is just as it had to be in arguments for toleration in a period of generalised religious persecution and before the acceptance of modern liberalism in the late seventeenth century.

Historically it can hardly be held that Christians tolerated other faiths. Christians regularly imposed belief through enforced mass conversion and crusades against religious dissenters.[8] The Muslim record in respecting the other religions of the Bible up to recent times is far better. Theologically, however, enforced belief is nonsense for modern Christians. Pierre Bayle, for example, in his commentary on the meaning of Jesus' injunction 'compel them to come in', argued that forced belief is worthless. Nominal conversion has no value if no genuine intention to come to Christ underlies it. Christians can only be true believers if they have uncoerced faith in Christ.[9]

Figgis clearly sets out that the religious argument against persecution cannot be based on the secular freedom of the individual in self-regarding actions. Christians cannot accept J. S. Mill's argument that one can go to hell in a handcart if what one has done reflects only on oneself. Figgis says society may legitimately prohibit acts such as drunkenness and gambling, because they both damage individuals and public order. But so too may a bad book, the committed religious activist may add. Individuals are formed in society and the individual's conscience is always partly social in its contents and workings. Why should not society protect people from bad ideas and form individuals in good ways? The answer turns on who is to judge. The real danger of the persecution that follows from enforced belief is that it reduces some to a position where their only role is obedience. This is fatal for an open and developing religious association. All religions need to change in doctrine and organisation to adapt to new conditions. Persecution rigorously followed prohibits new ideas and, therefore, development and innovation. A religion based on the choice of the individual to come to Christ and on individual moral responsibility cannot rigidly enforce belief. For all the legitimate claims of authority both religious and secular, 'in the last resort the individual must decide, and persecution denies this' (Figgis 1913 p. 117).

Toleration and criticism need not diminish faith, rather for the committed among the religious it will strengthen and reinforce it. Figgis is a definite advocate of the maxim, 'better fewer but better', so much so that he would have liked to see the Church of England disestablished so that it would be free to govern itself without being forced to accept compromises with mainstream opinion by the state, and so that it could accept only genuine believers, and not everyone who happened to want to get married or buried with some ceremony. The danger of an established church was rather, like that of persecution, it led not to heightened faith but to mediocrity. Ultimate 'you cannot do more than establish the ideals of the man in the street' (Figgis 1913 p. 114).

Figgis thus produced a religious defence of secularism and toleration. This was quite unlike that offered in Mill's *On Liberty*, for the defence of the freedom to innovate is couched in religious terms. Figgis' liberalism is ultimately a Christian liberalism, founded on an interpretation of what it means to come to Christ. Individual freedom is seen in theological terms as well as sociologically and prudentially. As we shall see later, Figgis saw in Ultramontanism the denial of this liberty and the adoption of an absolutist conception of sovereignty within the Catholic Church's government. Thus the argument is not just a backup to secular ones, but implies a definite stance on how churches should be governed.

Plurality and Prudence

Given our current discontents and the claims of the fanatically religious, it is essential that there be arguments that defend secularism in theological terms and individual liberty in terms of the character of church government. Those arguments are not directed at the invincibly ignorant among the fundamentalists, most of whom are also impervious to theological argument of any subtlety. However, purely secular arguments for a neutral state are inadequate to address those who think primarily and legitimately within a specific religious idiom. Understanding toleration from a theological stand-point and understanding that liberty of conscience is a part of church government in the Christian tradition are ways of building commitments to the secular state conceived in the narrow sense. In a similar vein, arguments for greater liberty in countries with Islamic regimes will certainly fail to gain wide acceptance if they are seen to depend on the reception of Western liberalism. The aim must be to renew and reinforce those arguments for a more tolerant style of governance of belief in Islamic theology and political tradition.

Arguments for toleration need to be rooted in definite national political and religious traditions and not seen as depending exclusively on the reception of 'universal' human rights. This is neither a matter of cultural relativism nor just a tactical matter of avoiding rights being perceived as an alien imposition. Genuine rights and liberties are always embedded in specific political traditions and carried by definite institutions.[10] If we are able to generalise politically from such specific contexts, it is because we can conceive such rights as what different nations and traditions have in common or provide in their distinctive contributions to the accepted common store of political wisdom. Toleration and liberty are values which are not the exclusive possession of Western secular liberals, and would be weaker as a political force on a world scale if that were so. It should also be clear that this is not a generalised relativist claim, some cultures and religions have little or nothing to contribute.

Religious liberty is not something external to religion that is granted to it by the state, it is a condition essential to the life and development of most religious groups themselves. This need the religious share with other associations. The freedom to develop within can only exist in the context of an appropriate political settlement without. Groups need their liberty to be secured both against excessive intrusion by the state and against the pretensions to hegemony of other groups. Autonomy can be preserved only if associations accept a double limitation: of the role of the state and of their own actions. As we have seen, in a society of competing religions limited government is a necessity, the state abstains from legislating conformity in religious belief and provides secular laws for those who are not religious. Religious groups need such limited government prudentially; a state that only interferes in religious matters to protect common rights. To have this prudential freedom groups must accept limitations on their belief and practice; they must internalise the prudential necessity that they not persecute as a positive value. The condition for viable religious pluralism is the vast majority of the religious accept that, whilst free to govern themselves, they are particular associations on a social scale. This involves placing core theology and the values governing practical action in different registers. Religions are able to compete for converts, if they wish. However, if a religion claims to be the one true faith and universal it must treat this as a perpetually deferred aspiration, part of ultimate belief rather than of current policy. Given the widespread acceptance of this double limitation by the religious (and, of course, by non-religious associations too), then a pluralist state overseeing a society of self-governing associations is sociologically possible.

Most religious groups accept this double limitation in matters of faith. For example, only a lunatic fringe of even the fundamentalist right in the USA believes that Catholics or Jews should be discriminated against. The problem is that, having accepted pluralism in belief, religious groups continue to struggle over a series of substitutes for religious authority in the sphere of conduct and social values. The only way to contain the conflicts arising from cultural heterogeneity is to extend the principle of pluralism from belief to conduct and to include in it the religious and non-religious. This would be to accept a plurality of rules, to let groups govern themselves side by side in matters of conduct.

Groups would have to give up trying to shape the laws that apply to all to suit their beliefs alone. They would exchange the ultimately futile struggle for dominance of the political agenda for the practice of governing themselves and competing to realise their beliefs about conduct by seeking members who will accept their rules in civil society. To say that would involve major sacrifices that powerful groups are unwilling to make is true, but that was even more the case with religious toleration in the first place. Faced with escalating conflicts over divergent social standards most groups may accept parallel governance as the least worst substitute.

The political solution to such conflicts would thus be to extend the scope of Figgis' conception of plural communities within a minimal secular state. Groups would be given the incentive of greater capacities for self-governance to accept this new settlement. Parallel governance could be furthered by giving both religious and secular groups a greater share in the control of welfare and other public services like education and health. Elsewhere, in *Associative Democracy*, I have argued for the reform of public services in terms of their provision by self-governing voluntary associations that are provided with public funds to do so proportionate to membership.[11] Individuals would have a periodic right to change and to exit the service provider they had elected to join. This would limit the power of groups and provide a primary check to inefficiency. Religious and non-religious groups would compete to offer the wider benefits of group membership. I have advanced these arguments for a wider variety of reasons than accommodating religious groups within a culturally diverse society. Nevertheless, the lure of public funds in return for the provision of services to their members would be likely to wed most groups to the pluralist principle, leaving only a tiny minority of fanatics who could be contained by the criminal law if they attempted violently to impose beliefs on others.

How would groups govern conduct in parallel? Two models present themselves, which I have developed in more detail elsewhere.[12] The first is micro-governance; that is, special territorial zones where different rules apply. Existing examples are the red light districts in the Netherlands, where prostitution is tolerated, or the Gay villages in many cities, like Manchester, where *de facto* different rules apply. The second is mutual extraterritoriality, that is the parallel existence of self-governing communities sharing the same space but applying rules in matters of community concern to their members alone. Examples of such practices are varied, from the Pillars system in the Netherlands to be Ottoman *millets* system. Plural governance is no utopian scheme, but has existed in different forms in many societies and cultures. Indeed, it might be said that it is the claim of the modern state to enforce legal and cultural homogeneity that is the exception. Historical examples abound of groups living side by side with a thin core of common rules and imposing their rules on themselves and nobody else.[13]

This means, of course, that people would have to concede the legitimate existence of practices they dislike. Fundamentalist Christians would have to accept the existence of a Gay community with its own rules, including marriage. Feminists would have to accept communities that gave men and women very different rights, like the Mormons. They would not have to submit to such practices themselves, but they would have to swallow their presence in the same society. On some issues, like abortion, this probably would not work, but for most conducts groups would evolve a frosty mutual tolerance.

Secular liberals might well be the group who would find this community self-governance most difficult to accept. Their problem is that, even in a state that supports secular values in education and culture, in the end strong communities will create their own institutions and try to sustain their beliefs within them. Hassids and Born Again Christians want to bring their children up like themselves. Only a rigorous secularist policy of enforced non-religious education could prevent this, but that would be illiberal. The key right that a pluralist state, based as it is on *voluntary* associations, would have to enforce and that would involve conflict with many groups is that of exit. Individuals must be supported by the law if groups try to impose excessive financial penalties on leaving or try to coerce their members to stay. A pluralist society would have a functionally limited public realm and a thin common culture; it would thus carry the liberal principles of neutrality and limited government beyond the point that many liberals would feel comfortable with. Pluralism of this kind will also upset communitarians who believe in a common thick script of values; here associations have the thick scripts (if that is what individuals want), not society as a whole. The problem for those who believe in a common substantive secular culture is that this fragmentation is already happening, people are beginning to live radically different lives. Associationalism preserves some of the core features of liberalism, but its is a distinct theory which side-steps the terms of the liberal-communitarian debate.

Figgis, Fellowship and Christianity

Figgis' political views were shaped in large measure by his religious commitments and so at least a limited account of some relevant aspects of his religious thought should be offered here. He sees Catholic Christianity as a community of believers united through the sacraments. It is a religion open to all and demands no special religious gifts: 'the Catholic Church is a religious democracy . . . It is a life for all, and not for some. No barrier but his own choice excludes any man. Its highest act of worship and of communion, the Eucharist, is shared by all; and the gift is the same to saint and sinner, to priest and layman, to archbishop and to an artisan' (Figgis 1914 p. 149). Figgis strongly attacks the Ultramontane doctrine of Papal absolutism. He sees this claim to rule the Church as identical to state sovereignty in its worst forms: 'If the whole government of a Church believed to exist by divine right is invested in one man, not as administrator but as lord; then since the Church is religious life, his infallibility is a logical corollary' (*ibid.*). Just as with the concessionist theory of associations, this doctrine results in 'the denial of all living reality to any other person or body within the Church' and the lay person has no 'right beyond obedience' (Figgis 1913 pp. 149–50).

This claim to unlimited sovereignty is more dangerous still within the Church than in the state, for in effect it denies that people are spiritual beings guided by their own conscience. Autocracy 'must destroy the springs of spiritual life in the individual conscience. Wherever blind obedience is preached, there is the danger of moral corruption.' (Figgis 1914 p. 154). The danger of Papal autocracy and the danger of spiritual aristocracy in certain Protestant sects are similar in that both downgrade the spiritual value, and, therefore the political contribution, of ordinary members of the church.

Figgis saw in Nietzsche the epitome of many of the faults of those fashionable ideas that sought to go beyond Christianity. He saw in Nietzsche's reception in Germany and his adoption by the powerful the anticipation of totalitarianism. He reminds us that the Kaiser presented Houston Stewart Chamberlain's *The Foundations of the Nineteenth Century* to his senior officers. Figgis condemned in the German leadership 'its worship of blind force, its contempt for all human values, its goal of a conquering full-blooded but disciplined aristocracy, governing with ruthless selfishness the vast mass of men, the herd of slave races' (Figgis 1917 p. xi). Even allowing for wartime propaganda, this depiction of the Wilhelmine elite is completely over the top, but it does serve as a remarkable anticipation of what Nazism stood for. Figgis understood and admired Nietzsche, but he saw the doctrine of the will-to-power as essentially pernicious.[14] In *The Will to Freedom or the Gospel of Nietzsche and the Gospel of Christ* Figgis attacked Nietzsche's claim that Christianity was fuelled by *ressentiment* and was the life-denying religion of the envious herd. Christianity is, on the contrary, a positive gospel of freedom and an invocation to 'live dangerously' as Christ did. The gospel of power and the gospel of freedom are different in essence: 'A gospel of Power must lead on the part of either the individual or class to a theory of egoism, of pride and of tyranny. It is in essence exclusive. A gospel of freedom, must equally of course lead to a doctrine of tolerance, of humility; for freedom implies the recognition of others—power pure and simple is satisfied to use them as tools' (Figgis 1917 p. 288).

Christianity represents fellowship, the will-to-power the worst of Pagan elitism and authoritarianism: 'The one doctrine separates the man or class or state in whom Power is vested from all others, and superimposes it on the rest. The other recognises leadership and rule, but as part of the membership 'one of another', which is the essence alike of citizenship and churchmanship' (Figgis 1917 p. 289). This neatly sums up Figgis' conception of the difference between legitimate authority and illegitimate power. The danger of unlimited sovereignty, whether in church or state, is that it dresses up force separated from society in the trappings of law. Figgis was thus a pluralist for both religious and secular political reasons, but it is difficult fully to appreciate the latter without the former.

Notes

1 See J. C. Isaac *et. al.* 'American democracy and the New Christian Right: a critique of apolitical liberalism,' in I. Shapiro and C. Hacker-Cordon, *Democracy's Edges*, Cambridge, Cambridge University Press, 1999.
2 See P. Hirst 'The International Origins of National Sovereignty', Ch. 14 of *From Statism to Pluralism*, London, UCL Press, 1997.
3 See H. Kamen, *The Rise of Toleration*, London, Weidenfeld and Nicolson, 1967.
4 The best account of Figgis' thought remains D. Nicholls, *The Pluralist State*, London, Macmillan. First edition 1975, second edition 1994. In many ways the first edition is still better, for Figgis' thought in particular. For a judicious account of the career of English political pluralist ideas in this century see R. Barker, 'Pluralism, Revenant or Recessive?' in J. Hayward, B. Barry and A. Brown, eds., *The British Study of Politics in the Twentieth Century*, London, The British Academy/Oxford University Press, 1999.
5 See J. N. Figgis *The Divine Right of Kings*, originally published 1914, second edition Cambridge, Cambridge University Press 1922; J. N. Figgis *Studies in Political Thought From Gerson to Grotius*, Cambridge, Cambridge University Press 1916; J. N. Figgis *The Political Aspects of St. Augustine's 'City of God'* London, Longmans, Green & Co., 1921.
6 Respectively: London, Longmans, Green & Co. 1913, second 1914 edition reprinted by Thoemmes Press, Bristol 1997; London, Longmans, Green & Co. 1914; London, Longmans, Green & Co., 1917.
7 In this respect D. Runciman's extensive study of the issue of corporate personality and political theory, *Pluralism and the Personality of the State* Cambridge, Cambridge University Press, 1998, is to my mind unsympathetically and irritatingly critical of Figgis.
8 For discussions of Christian expansion and the suppression of heresy by armed force in Europe see respectively, R. Fletcher, *The Conversion of Europe: From paganism to Christianity 371–1386 AD*, London, Fontana, 1998 and N. Housley

The Later Crusades: From Lyons to Alcazar 1274–1580, Oxford, Oxford University Press, 1992.

9 For a succinct introduction to Bayle's thought see E. Labrousse, *Bayle*, Oxford, Oxford University Press, 1983.

10 Some idea of the issues at stake can be gained from considering the hostile English reaction to the claim of the French revolutionaries to represent universal human rights, summed up in Edmund Burke's defence of the specific English tradition of liberty as embodied in its own distinctive institutions in *Reflections on the Revolution in France*.

11 Cambridge, Polity Press, 1994.

12 See 'Statism, Pluralism and Social Control' in a special issue of *The British Journal of Criminology* on 'Criminology and Social Theory' 2000.

13 This existence of parallel communities is discussed in another quite distinct English pluralist tradition, that represented by the anthropologists J. S. Furnivall and M. G. Smith. See M. G. Smith 'Institutional and Political Conditions of Pluralism' in his *Corporations and Society*, London, Duckworth, 1974. The approach advocated here to problems of cultural homogeneity is not the only possible one and different solutions have been advanced. Some arguments emphasise the strong legal protection of minorities, for a rigorous example see, W. Kymlicka, *Multicultural Citizenship: A Liberal Theory of Minority Rights*, Oxford, Clarendon Press, 1995. For a different approach that questions some of the basic liberal assumptions see, J. Gray, *Enlightenment's Wake: Politics and Culture at the Close of the Modern Age*, London, Routledge, 1995. Space prevents a discussion here as I have concentrated on the exposition of Figgis' ideas.

14 This is not the place to discuss how accurate Figgis' account of Nietzsche is; he could not be aware of the later controversies surrounding the editing of the notes that form *The Will to Power*. The point of citing Figgis' views is less the accuracy of his interpretation, although he was aware that Nietzsche had nothing but contempt for German nationalism, than the power-centred political attitude that he criticises, which was a very real threat to the idea of freedom for all and not just the elite.

Making the Christian World Safe for Liberalism: From Grotius to Rawls

TIMOTHY SAMUEL SHAH

Pluralism, Liberalism, History

Anyone familiar with the books Anglo-American political scientists write, the seminars they run, or the conferences they organise will know that two distinct sets of questions preoccupy Anglo-American political science today.

One set of questions arises from concern about *pluralism*: What is the most appropriate political response to the pluralism or 'difference' of all kinds—religious, cultural, moral—that obtains in many of the world's societies? In particular, how is it politically possible simultaneously to respect pluralism and contain the radical conflict pluralism threatens? The other set of questions arises from concern about *liberalism* as a distinct mode of political theory and practice: What is, or should be, the non-negotiable 'core' of liberalism? Should purely political principles and procedures, formulated and justified independently of morality, philosophy, and religion, constitute liberalism's core? Or is liberalism something more substantive?

In this chapter I take up these questions by examining their point of intersection: How do—and should—pluralism and liberalism interrelate? Are liberalism's principles and procedures appropriate to societies characterised by radical pluralism? If not, must liberalism be adjusted to match the reality of pluralism? Or must pluralism somehow be adjusted to match the aspirations and structures of liberalism? I approach these questions through a chiefly historical inquiry: What can we learn about how pluralism and liberalism can and should interrelate from the history of their interrelationship? In particular, I focus on a foundational moment in this history.

According to Judith Shklar, liberalism emerged as a response to the religious conflicts of the 16th and 17th centuries: 'liberalism is a latecomer, since it has its origins in post-Reformation Europe. Its origins are in the terrible tension within Christianity between the demands of creedal orthodoxy and those of charity, between faith and morality.'[1] The context in which liberalism emerged, in other words, was precisely one of radical pluralism. Specifically, liberalism emerged from within a divided and conflicted Christianity, split asunder by the Reformation. Once Christendom was divided into a plurality of confessions each of which claimed exclusive authority, the question for European Christians became: 'How can we (Christians) of (any) one confession treat rival confessions and their members in a way that is faithful to the law of Christ—a law that demands, simultaneously, absolute fidelity to Christ's Truth and absolute obedience to Christ's Love?' It did not

© The Political Quarterly Publishing Co. Ltd. 2000
Published by Blackwell Publishers, 108 Cowley Road, Oxford OX4 1JF, UK and 350 Main Street, Malden, MA 02148, USA

seem that fidelity to his Truth could be reconciled with heresy and disunity, but neither did it seem that obedience to his Love could be reconciled with inquisitions and religious warfare. In a divided Christendom, how could Christians reconcile Truth and Love, 'orthodoxy' and 'morality'?

The great Dutch polymath Hugo Grotius (1583–1645) took the challenge of post-Reformation radical pluralism to heart. His response, I believe, laid the central conceptual foundations for liberalism and is thus crucial for under-standing the subsequent interrelationship of pluralism and liberalism in the West.

My historical inquiry pursues two questions: (1) What is the relationship between pluralism and liberalism? In particular, to what extent is there a *characteristically liberal* response to the challenge of *religious* pluralism? (2) To the extent that there is, is it adequate? My approach is to sketch an answer to each of these questions by way of a highly limited survey of the history of liberal political thought. I begin at the 'beginning' of the story with Hugo Grotius, and then (after a brief glance at John Locke) turn quickly to the 'end' of the story (i.e., the present) by looking at the greatest living Anglo-American political philosopher, John Rawls. I examine Rawls alongside Grotius to see whether these very different liberals in very different (though in some respects interestingly similar) circumstances nonetheless adopt a common, characteristic approach to pluralism.

First, pluralism and liberalism in Hugo Grotius. To borrow Shklar's categories, Grotius' response to religious pluralism was to quell religious conflict by reducing 'orthodoxy' to 'morality'. On the basis of a new orthodoxy of common morality, he sought to show Christians of diverse confessions that their moral agreements were more theologically significant than their doctrinal disagreements. Grotius—anticipating Rawls, as it were—thus introduced what became a characteristically liberal response to the challenge of pluralism: that of an 'overlapping consensus' of diverse world-views around a minimal, non-metaphysical morality. However, only if a preponderance of Christian confessions could accept Grotius' radical redefi-nition of orthodoxy—indeed, his radical re-definition of Christianity itself—could his consensus win wide allegiance. Therefore, Grotius could make his liberal response to religious pluralism effective only by containing religious pluralism within the narrow bounds of his new orthodoxy. With Grotius' new conception of orthodoxy came a new conception of heterodoxy, which univocally considered all systems of Christian belief incompatible with Grotian orthodoxy a threat to liberalism. In the category of anti-liberal heterodoxy Grotius above all included Calvinism, against whose influence he worked tirelessly as well as (in part) successfully. In promoting his liberal and widely influential overlapping consensus, Grotius helped make the Christian world safe for liberalism but unsafe for religious pluralism.

Secondly, I discuss John Rawls's liberal response to religious pluralism in *Political Liberalism* (1993, 1996) and suggest that he, too, in seeking to keep the world safe for liberalism in effect makes it unsafe for religious pluralism. In a way that is remarkably similar to Grotius, Rawls also can make his liberal response to religious pluralism effective only by containing religious pluralism within the narrow bounds of 'reasonableness,' the basis of his consensual political morality. An anti-pluralist containment strategy, which univocally presumes certain religious beliefs as such to be incompatible with liberalism, thus continues to mark the liberal response to pluralism. For a more sound response to the challenge of pluralism in today's world, we must look beyond the tradition of 'Grotian' liberalism.

The Containment of Religious Pluralism within Grotian Bounds

If Grotius is a crucial part of the story of how a characteristically liberal response to religious pluralism developed, it is above all because he undertook the noble task of persuading Europeans of diverse and incommensurable religious points of view that religious division was not an evil but something they *could and should* live with. We can best understand Grotius' persuasive efforts by situating them in their tumultuous historical context.

The Protestant Reformation had a profound and politically unsettling effect on Grotius' own United Provinces. In the latter half of the 16th century, Calvinism spread to the Low Countries, which at that time were under Spanish (i.e., Catholic) rule. In 1568, violent resistance to Spain, led by the Calvinists, triggered an eight-year struggle for independence. While officially Calvinist since 1572, the United Provinces soon experienced dispute as to what range of theological opinion an established Calvinism should tolerate. With the conclusion of a truce with Spain in 1609, this dispute intensified and polarized.

On one side were 'orthodox' Calvinists who demanded that the government impose uniformity within the official Reformed church and suppress or at least restrict religious groups—Catholics, Jews, and Protestant dissenters—outside the church. On the other side were the 'Remonstrants,' followers of Jacob Arminius: they disputed Calvinist predestinarianism, believed that the state church should be under government authority as well as broadly inclusive, and argued that the government should tolerate those outside the church. The rivalry widened to include the two pre-eminent political leaders of the United Provinces, Johan von Oldenbarnevelt, executive secretary of the States General of the United Provinces and effectively head of government, and Prince Maurice, *de facto* head of state. After 1609 Prince Maurice increasingly sided with the orthodox Calvinists; Oldenbarnevelt, appalled by religious extremism, leaned toward the Remonstrants.

The young Grotius became a close associate of Oldenbarnevelt, eventually becoming one of Rotterdam's representatives to the States-General. Believing on principle in a wide toleration and more inclusive Christianity (as we shall see), Grotius joined Oldenbarnevelt in opposing the orthodox Calvinists. By

1618, however, a majority of the States-General favoured the orthodox Calvinists, and the opposition of Oldenbarnevelt and Grotius was more and more widely interpreted as both heterodox and treasonous. After seizing the government in a *coup d'état*, Prince Maurice had them both arrested and tried for treason, and they were swiftly found guilty. In one of the two most spectacular political executions of the 17th century (the second would of course come almost precisely thirty years later), Oldenbarnevelt, at the age of 71, was beheaded in May 1619. Grotius was sentenced to life imprisonment— though he made a dramatic escape and eventually found his way to Paris, where he spent most of the rest of his life.

To appreciate the ingenuity of Grotius' liberal approach to religious pluralism, it is first crucial to understand the profound conceptual reasons why the people involved in the religious conflicts of the 16th and 17th centuries could not have found liberalism an acceptable (or in some cases even an imaginable) response to their situation. For the barriers to the rise of liberalism were in key part conceptual. To become religiously tolerant, in other words, what the age of Grotius needed was far more than mere hard historical 'experience' or 'exhaustion', but to overcome conceptual barriers. Experience, by itself, is mute, and exhaustion temporary. Neither, by itself, could have induced more than a temporary resignation to religious diversity, far short of reconciliation to it as something acceptable. It is thus a mistake to think that the sheer experience of religious conflict 'taught' Europe and the world the lesson of liberalism. The experience of religious conflict taught the anti-tolerationists John Calvin, Justus Lipsius, Jean Bodin, and the Roman Catholic Church no such thing. An identical experience often teaches different people quite different things, and the religious diversity of post-Reformation Europe was particularly susceptible to a plethora of incompatible perceptions. Diverse theological perceptions, according to which religious diversity was conceived not as something to be lived with, but as something to be stamped out, and political-theoretical perceptions, according to which it was literally inconceivable that a religiously divided society could be stable, thus constituted high conceptual barriers to liberalism.

Try, for example, to see the religious conflict of the 17th-century United Provinces from the point of view of an engaged participant such as an earnest Calvinist Reformer: you are trying to shore up an incipient and threatened movement whose mission is to purify Christ's church and make every societal sphere conform to Christ's laws. From your point of view 'religious diversity' is no bare 'sociological' fact. Rather, you see religious diversity *qua* 'threat to the survival of Reform and hence to the purity of the true church,' and thus *qua* 'evil as such,' to which one and only one remedy is appropriate, namely, state enforcement of Calvinist orthodoxy. If you are a Jesuit, seeking to restore the *consensus fidelium*, firmly and universally maintained across the centuries until shattered by obstinate schismatics, again you do not see religious diversity as a bare sociological fact, but instead *qua* 'schism and the dissemination of heresy,' to which one and only one solution is appropriate, namely, a re-united Christendom under the Pope. On the other hand, if you are a Neo-Stoic humanist like Lipsius, you do not see religious diversity as having any transcendent religious significance, but *qua* 'sheer disorder' and 'threat to political unity,' for, as Lipsius put it, 'from a confused religion there always groweth dissension.' A Lipsius, moved not by religious zeal but political necessity, considered it imperative to destroy religious dissent and impose a uniform public religion wherever possible.

In examining these different responses to religious diversity, each of which had many devoted adherents in the 16th and 17th centuries, notice the *conception-dependent* character of each position's perception of religious diversity. The nature of religious diversity is that it consists in deep disagreement not only about fundamental questions of doctrine—e.g., Is the Pope the Vicar of Christ or the Anti-Christ?—but about *how to conceptualize religious diversity itself*. Religious diversity may be a fact, but the socially and politically relevant question is: How do we evaluate its *significance*? What does it *mean*? How we answer these questions and thus how we perceive the fact of religious diversity depends just as much on our basic religious conception as how we answer a fundamental question of doctrine. In other words, our interpretation of the fact of religious diversity seems to be just as conception-dependent as our assessment of, for example, the claim that the Pope is the Vicar of Christ.

Furthermore, these responses to religious diversity were not merely different, but *mutually incommensurable*—just as much as their conceptions of one another's fundamental doctrinal claims. For example, even to describe post-Reformation Europe in seemingly neutral terms as characterised by 'a diversity of religions' places Catholicism and Calvinism on a par in a way that neither the Calvinist nor the Catholic of the time could have accepted. And the mutual incommensurability of these religious traditions' proposed *solutions* to the problem of religious division is obvious. In other words, when religious disputants turn from the fundamental issues of disagreement to the fact of disagreement itself, they are not suddenly looking at anything any less controversial. The great barrier to developing a common approach to the problem of religious conflict, therefore, was (and remains) that there was (and is) no neutral way of perceiving even the 'fact' of religious diversity, much less any given solution. Religious diversity could thus become acceptable to the variety of mutually hostile religious confessions of the time, and hence something to which they could reconcile themselves, only if they could come to understand it in a new theological light—specifically, if they could come to see it *under a fresh, commonly accessible, and shared theological description*.

Making Religion Peaceable by Making Religion Moral

When Hugo Grotius sat down to write a theological treatise in 1610, at the height of religious controversy in the United Provinces, he believed he could present an account of Christianity that would be recognised as valid by diverse religious confessions, and at the same time radically transform how they conceived of religious diversity: far from being an evil of one sort or another, he believed he could show that it was an acceptable state of affairs. Given the dependence of these conceptions of religious diversity on fundamental theological doctrine, however, Grotius could not transform them without undertaking to transform Christianity itself.

Grotius' treatise was the *Meletius sive de iis quae inter Christianos conveniunt epistola* [*Meletius* or *Letter on the Points of Agreement between Christians*].[2] Occasioned by Grotius' horror of the mutual animosity and even violent conflict that had become so prevalent among European Christians, including Christians in the United Provinces, the *Meletius* begins with an observation on the ironic fact that 'in our age and in that of our fathers . . . not only indifference or rivalry, but also implacable hatred and anger, indeed—something almost unprecedented—wars are started under no other pretext than that of the very religion [i.e., Christianity] whose purpose is peace' (¶2). In the *Meletius* Grotius not only identifies the points of agreement between Christians of all sects and denominations, but, more importantly and radically, argues that what Christians share is *far more important from a theological point of view* than what they do not. In this work Grotius sought to do nothing less than to give Christianity a new centre of gravity, replacing dogma and creed with a morality oriented to social peace: a religion of other-wordly salvation would be moulded to fit the needs of deeply divided societies and thus re-described as 'the very religion whose purpose is peace.'

The foundation of Grotius' ecumenical scheme is his distinction between theological doctrines (*decreta*) and practical precepts (*praecepta*). According to this distinction, the sole point of *decreta* is to support *praecepta*. This distinction Grotius straightforwardly applies to religion:

Now religion, since it concerns those actions prompted by free will, all of which, however, are pre-determined by the intellect, necessarily consists of two parts, theoretical and practical. The former is made up of doctrines, the latter of ethical precepts . . . Doctrines should be active in every field of science and not be irrelevant or redundant, but should either incite to action or to some extent make clear what must be done and how it must be done (¶19).

Applying this distinction to *Christianity* in particular, he argues that *Christian* dogmas should be reduced to those necessary for ethics: otherwise, there is occasion for *needless* controversy. And the foundation of his view that controversy about Christian dogma is needless is not scepticism: he fiercely opposed scepticism in ethics and religion, as is evident in many of his works. Rather, it is founded on his confident claim that the fundamental part of religion is ethics: 'Many [religious] controversies over dogmas are merely due to words which must be avoided for *consensus* to appear. With any further quarrels we have to check whether they concern matters which it is necessary to know. At this point *we have, first of all, to correct the error that generally more dogmas are formulated than ethics require'* [my emphasis] (¶90). The solution to the problem of superfluous dogma consists in 'limiting the number of necessary articles of faith to those few that are most self-evident' (¶91).

Grotius' proposal is radical. If what 'it is necessary to know' is limited to those theological dogmas that 'ethics require,' theology effectively becomes a hand-maiden to ethics, and ethics displaces theology as the queen of the sciences. Grotius thus specifically and self-consciously sought to promote an inter-Christian 'consensus'—note his use of precisely this word—focused around ethical precepts elevated to a pre-eminent place. To facilitate the establishment of this overlapping consensus, Grotius encourages a parsimonious Christianity, reduced to its ethically relevant essentials. The outcome of the Grotian reduction of Christian dogma to the requirements of ethics may rightly be called 'religion within the limits of morality alone,' and this reduction indeed seems to anticipate the similar Kantian reduction of Christian dogma to rational morality.

But which few articles of faith are 'most self-evident'? In answering this question, the 'Kantian' character of Grotius' argument comes further into view. For he additionally argues that ethics is prior to dogma not only in importance, but *epistemically*. Ethics comes first not only in that it is in effect the point of theology, but also in that it is grasped with greater certainty: ethical precepts in fact are the 'most self-evident' elements of Christian faith. Indeed, this fact enables *praecepta* to play a regulative function in relation to *decreta*: from the firm ground of *praecepta* the necessity of the various *decreta* is assessed. Grotius makes a distinction among *praecepta* that demonstrates that not all *praecepta* are equally unequivocal but at the same time confirms that moral rules are uncontroversial in a way that religious dogmas are not:

Now when there is a fight over precepts, it hardly ever involves ethics—for those have definite and unequivocal rules—but deals with those matters which everybody establishes for himself for the sake of preserving order, and in which a short cut to concord is to leave every man to his own discretion . . . For how often did not at some time in the past dissensions arise from the fact that Easter was celebrated on different days by different people? (¶90)

Specifically moral *praecepta* Grotius describes in the *Meletius* as including, above all, charity, along with respect for matrimony, temperance, as well as the duties to God taught by all religions, such as public worship and prayer. These moral *praecepta* alone follow 'definite and unequivocal rules.' *Praecepta* regarding the details of ecclesiastical polity and liturgy, on the other hand, are variable and relatively unimportant, 'rank second in importance to those rules which describe the duties of love,' and are thus to be left to the discretion of Christians and their communities for the sake of 'concord.'

Among the most radical teachings of John Locke, his 1685 *Letter Concerning Toleration*, addressed to his friend Philip von Limborch while a political exile in Amsterdam, says in its first sentence: 'I esteem that Toleration to be the chief Characteristical mark of the True Church.' Anticipating Locke by some seventy-five years, Grotius makes a similar teaching the core doctrine of the *Meletius*:

No reason for discord [among Christians] can be so important that it would not be surpassed by that very reason for concord, to wit that we follow a single teacher, indeed *him who acknowledges no disciplines but those who devote themselves to concord* [my emphasis]. That is why, in the face of new conflicts every day and ever-regenerating disturbances, I usually find solace and new strength by reflecting on those things which God's goodness has kept intact for the Christians to this day; things which, by virtue of their being the greatest, the most certain and the most valuable, naturally mean so much to me that while I consider them, I put aside for the time being the other things which are of minor importance, less certain and less valuable. May these privileges, if I may call them that, at least prove to us that we are citizens of *one* community [Grotius' emphasis] (¶3).

If the true followers of Christ are those who 'devote themselves to concord,' the chief mark of true Christianity has in effect become 'peaceableness,' which amounts to much the same thing as Locke's 'toleration.' More likely, however, it amounts to something even more radical. For Grotius' comprehensive, peaceable Christianity most certainly included Catholics, whereas Locke's toleration did not. In what sense Grotius' peaceable Christianity could include atheists, which Locke's toleration also excludes, can be seen in the most famous passage of Grotius' *De iure belli ac pacis* [*On the Law of War and Peace*] (1625). After showing that individuals, simply by reflecting on their social nature, are capable of apprehending principles of natural law sufficient for establishing a peaceful social order, Grotius goes on to say that '[w]hat we have been saying would have a degree of validity even if we should concede [*etiamsi daremus*] that which cannot be conceded without the utmost wicked-ness, that there is no God, or that the affairs of men are of no concern to Him.'[3] The moral truths at the heart of the Christian consensus are essentially accessible not just to non-Christian believers, but to atheists.

Combining Grotius' foundational claims about the priority of moral precept to religious dogma with the claims of the above passage concerning concord leaves no doubt about what features of Christianity Grotius considered 'the greatest, the most certain, and the most valuable'—namely, its moral precepts, along with those theological dogmas that in some way support them. Once Grotius had reductionistically 'moralized' Christianity in this way, the extent to which even atheists could join Grotius' overlapping Christian consensus is remarkable—suggesting that very little distinctively Christian remains of Christianity once confined within Grotian bounds. The Grotian consensus of 'Christians' seems well on its way to the Rawlsian political not meta-physical consensus of the 'reasonable.'

The aid Grotius' theological work offers to liberalism is unmistakable. If Christians could take this theological re-description of their differences to heart, significant motives to impose religious uniformity and destroy liberty of conscience would disappear. More than that, a positive theological motive to respect other Christians—since to be a Christian *is in essence* to love concord—would be established; hatred and even (mere) tolerance would give way to a sense of shared citizenship in the *'one* [Christian] community' (¶3, quoted above). Religious diversity would not disappear: doctrinal distinctions among Calvinists, Catholics, and Arminians, and others, would remain. But these different Christians, Grotius hoped, would come to see their doctrinal diversity as *relatively insignificant, and thus come to see one another as essentially* co-religionists. If Christians could come to see that their highest calling is concord and that their points of agreement concern the greatest things, then Christianity would become peaceableness itself, paving the way for deep and effective religious toleration.

Less obvious, though directly related, is that the ultimate effect of Grotius' theological re-description is the flattening of genuine pluralism. While the theological scheme of Grotius' *Meletius* allows for ongoing confessional differences, a little reflection suggests that its widespread acceptance would cause over time the weakening of Christian sects centrally defined by beliefs or doctrines lying outside of Grotius' moralised Christianity. Think of Catholicism, for example. If Catholics were to come to accept Grotius' view of Christianity, Catholicism, with its distinctive and constitutive doctrines on 'peripheral,' non-ethical matters (i.e., church authority and structure), would essentially collapse into Protestantism—or at least Grotius' version of it—even though it might persist in a nominal form. In a letter to his moderate Calvinist friend Antonius Walaeus concerning the *Meletius*, Grotius revealingly indicates that if his conception of Christianity gained currency, this is exactly what would happen to 'Papism': '[I]t follows that if Religion is reduced to what all Christian churches at all times have believed in, then Papism collapses, for it is made up of isolated opinions.' What Grotius failed to point out to his Calvinist friend is that Calvinism—or any Christian sect defined by 'isolated opinions,' which for Grotius included predestination—would collapse for the same reason.[4]

But did Grotius really *intend* to contain or isolate Calvinism and hence limit religious pluralism in order to advance a liberal political agenda? In almost his last theological work, Grotius shows that he had long believed that for the essentials of liberalism to be secured, theological systems like Calvinism had to be changed if not destroyed. When Grotius was rebuked by a Leiden theologian for having given insufficient credit to the Calvinists for their role in the revolt against Spain, he shot back, pointing first to Prince Maurice's Calvinist *coup* of 1618 and then to the instigation by Calvin himself of the burning of the anti-Trinitarian heretic Michael Servetus in 1553:

William the Silent said that there were two reasons for the Revolt: safeguarding the constitution and liberty of conscience. The constitution was never so openly violated by the Spaniards as by Calvin's followers in 1618, at the instigation of the ministers . . . Liberty of conscience was safeguarded not only by the writings of Prince William, but by the Pacification of Ghent . . . and later by the Union of Utrecht, and by many other agreements made with particular cities; all true Calvinists are professed enemies to such liberty, as is shown by what happened to [Michael] Servetus at Calvin's hands.[5]

Grotius was deeply persuaded that Calvinism and liberalism were utterly incompatible. Being an earnest partisan of republican self-government, constitutionalism, and liberty of conscience, he therefore made the task of weakening 'true' Calvinism one of the defining projects of his life. As he put it with astonishing candour in another place: 'Those who seek to further peace among Christians are obliged to *destroy* those dogmas that disturb political peace' [my emphasis].[6]

Grotius was obviously not unjustified in regarding Calvinism with suspicion, given its intolerant record (and given his own hard treatment at the hands of his Calvinist countrymen). At the same time, Grotius' image of it was harshly univocal: he should have been aware that the Calvinism of his time was several generations removed from that of Calvin, and that even some of Calvin's contemporary followers had had misgivings about Servetus' execution. In any case, there was arguably no distinctively *Calvinist* basis for the idea that the state's duty was to enforce religious uniformity; this was a virtually universal conviction from the time of Constantine. Indeed, some Calvinists in the 16th and 17th centuries had begun to reconsider the question of religious toleration. Before undertaking to 'destroy'—and thus antagonize—Calvinism, Grotius should thus have been more open to its increasing 'multi-vocality,' its potential for immanent transformation, and hence the fact that 'all true Calvinists' *as such* need not have remained 'professed enemies' of liberty.[7]

Grotius' Liberal Legacy

Though Grotius circulated the *Meletius* among friends—one of whom rightly appraised it as 'entirely novel'—he feared that, given the acrimony of the theological controversy of the time, it would fan the flames of theological conflict. He therefore decided not to publish it. Still, its ideas proved spectacularly influential.

First, it laid the groundwork for a theological work Grotius did publish, which became wildly popular throughout Europe, the *De veritate religionis christianae* [*On the Truth of the Christian Religion*] (1627). Jean Le Clerc, an eighteenth-century editor and vigorous promoter of Grotian theology, describes its aim in accurate and revealing terms: '[T]he main object of [the *De veritate*] is to place in a clear light the truth of the Gospel, totally unconnected with the bias of any party or sect whatsoever; and that solely with a view to generate virtue, evangelical virtue, in the minds of men.' For the sake of consensus, the 'truth of the Christian religion' again comes to consist primarily in Christian morality. In fact, the *De veritate* was sharply criticized throughout the 17th century for failing even to *mention* such fundamental theological doctrines as the Trinity and the Atonement.

The influence of the *De veritate* was stunning. During Grotius' lifetime five translations appeared—an English translation, two German translations, and two French translations—and its posthumous success was overwhelming. No

© The Political Quarterly Publishing Co. Ltd. 2000

less than 144 Latin and translated editions have been published since 1645 (including at least one Welsh edition, a copy of which is in the Bodleian). In the 17th century its influence was immense, in the United Provinces as well as in England; after the Restoration, Anglican bishops and theologians had an extremely high regard for it. In the same period, in 1663–1664, a young Censor of Moral Philosophy at Christ Church, John Locke, was recommending the *De veritate* to his students. In Grotius' lifetime it had already become known as the 'golden booklet.' As famous as his 1625 international law-book would soon become, Grotius was in his own century undoubtedly better known as the author of the *De veritate* than *De iure belli ac pacis*. Given Grotius' ambition to make religious diversity theologically acceptable to Christians of diverse points of view, this was the popularity for which he would have dreamed.

Secondly, though the *Meletius* was unpublished, a copy ended up in the hands of Philip von Limborch, the great Dutch Arminian theologian. Limborch of course became a close friend of John Locke during the latter's exile in Holland and was the original recipient of Locke's *Letter Concerning Toleration*. Interestingly, there are strong resemblances between Limborch's *Theologia Christiana* (1686)—which almost certainly influenced Locke's later *Reasonableness of Christianity* (1695)—and the *Meletius*.

Thirdly, there is good reason to believe that the *Meletius* paved the way for religious toleration in this more definite sense: it probably had a direct influence on Locke before and during his composition of his *Letter Concerning Toleration*. We have already noted one instance of substantial agreement between the two works that would suggest this influence. A further instance is the prominent place each work gives to the radical teaching that even heretical beliefs can be salvific so long as they are sincerely held.[8] If there were an influence, an explanation of how it might have occurred is obvious, given the close connection between Limborch and Locke (Locke came to regard Limborch as the 'best of friends' and the 'best of men'), which began in 1684. Given the length of Locke's stay in Holland (1683–1689) and the closeness of Locke's association with Limborch throughout this period it is probable that Locke was at some point exposed to the *Meletius*. Indeed, it seems almost impossible that in frequent theological discussions Limborch could have refrained from discussing Grotius' treatise—especially given Locke's documented interest in Grotius' *De veritate* while at Oxford, an interest Locke would have had ample occasion to mention.

Whatever the exact connection between Grotius and Locke, there is astonishing evidence that within fifty years of his death, Grotius' religious writings, particularly the *De veritate*, were having their intended impact on Christianity in general and on Calvinism in particular. In 1676, the Genevan pastor Pierre Mussard was sent into exile by Geneva's orthodox Calvinists because of his belief in universal salvation. He subsequently went to London, where he was delighted by what he found: London's choice of theological authorities had come to diverge dramatically from Geneva's. Writing to a Genevan friend, Mussard noted that in London '[p]oor Calvin is extremely odious' and that 'Grotius has acquired all the esteem here that one used to have for Calvin. I have even found that Grotius is cited from the pulpit with the accolade "divine" and "incomparable."' By the beginning of the 18th century, hardly a generation later, Grotius' influence had widened yet further: a profound admiration for Grotius became evident among theologians in—of all places—Geneva. The vehemently critical reaction of Calvinist theologians to this trend is telling: the Calvinist Elie Merlat, for example, professor of theology at the Académie de Lausanne, hotly opposed the widespread adoration of the 'incomparable' Grotius among his fellow theologians in Geneva. In 1704, when a Genevan theologian had insisted in a letter to Merlat that he did not know anyone who would refuse Grotius the most fulsome praise, Merlat fired back:

I have proof in may hands of the impiety of Grotius, and of his mocking spirit towards holy things; and his treatise on the *Truth of the Christian Religion* is not at all capable of exculpating him in this regard, but can even serve to convince one of this . . . I am sure of what I say, that never was there a man, in my view, either so learned as Grotius, or so great a corrupter of the Christian religion . .

The Containment of Religious Pluralism within Rawlsian Bounds

Someone might object, however: Did the liberal solution to the problem of religious pluralism really *require* the anti-pluralist containment—'corruption'—of Christianity along Grotian lines? Has liberalism remained committed to, and does it really require, a narrow containment of religious pluralism?

Rawls's liberal response to religious pluralism begins in agitation—an agitation about Christianity that recalls Grotius' agitation about Calvinism. In a new 'Introduction' to *Political Liberalism*, Rawls clarifies the 'fundamental philosophical' question his liberal political theory has been seeking to answer: 'How is it possible for those affirming a *religious doctrine* that is based on *religious authority*, for example, the Church or the Bible, *also* to hold a *reasonable* political conception that supports a *just democratic* regime? . . . How is it possible for citizens of *faith* to be *wholehearted* members of a *democratic* society . . .' [my emphasis].[9] People who accept the authority of 'the Church or the Bible'—i.e. Christians *as such*—pose (are?) a fundamental political problem. For just on the basis of what they believe, Rawls considers Christians *qua* Christians a presumptive threat: note his presumed opposition between 'religious doctrine,' 'religious authority,' and 'faith,' on the one hand, and 'reasonable,' 'just,' and 'democratic,' on the other. The barely implicit starting-point of Rawls's liberalism is the question, 'How is it possible' that such (irreconcilable) things be reconciled? More explicit are Rawls's univocal and elaborate statements about 'the Christian religion' in his most recent publication, in which he insists that its 'great curse' has been a 'persecuting zeal' and that its 'dreadful evils' are comparable to—indeed partly responsible for—the 'demonic madness' of Hitler's Holocaust.[10]

In other words, Rawls's agitation about Christianity is similar not only to Grotius' univocal agitation about 17th century Calvinism, but to Samuel Huntington's much-discussed univocal agitation about late-twentieth-century Islam: 'The underlying problem for the West is not Islamic fundamentalism. It is Islam . . '[11] The underlying problem for Rawlsian liberalism is not Christian fundamentalism. It is Christianity.

Given Rawls's formulation of the underlying problem, it is not surprising that he considers the containment of presumptively unreasonable and illiberal religion—Christianity always being his paradigm case—an essential component of liberalism. To see that he regards the constraint of religious pluralism as necessary to liberalism's success, note first his revealing discussion of liberalism's historical development:

[T]he success of liberal constitutionalism came as a discovery of a new social possibility: the possibility of a reasonably harmonious and stable pluralist society. Before the successful and peaceful practice of toleration in societies with liberal institutions there was no way of knowing of that possibility. It is more natural to believe, as the centuries-long practice of intolerance appeared to confirm, that social unity and concord requires agreement on a general and comprehensive religious, philosophical, or moral doctrine. Intolerance was accepted as a condition of social order and stability. The weakening of that belief helps to clear the way of liberal institutions. Perhaps the doctrine of free faith developed because *it is difficult, if not impossible, to believe in the damnation of those with whom we have, with trust and confidence, long and fruitfully cooperated in maintaining a just society* [my emphasis] (xxvii).

Certain religious beliefs—belief that (some of) one's fellow citizens are (or may be) damned to hell, for example—Rawls does not consider compatible with liberalism. Their gradual passing away, far from being regrettable, cleared the way for liberalism.

Rawls thus demonstrates his agreement with Grotius that certain religious beliefs stand in the way of liberalism and, whether by direct persuasion or gradual attenuation, have to be overcome 'to clear the way for liberal institutions.' Note that Rawls's example is a belief that is not political as such and in no clear way runs counter to liberal ideals: *contra* Rawls (as well as Rousseau, whose *Social Contract* [IV.viii] Rawls is implicitly following here), it hardly follows from one's believing in the doctrine of eternal damnation that one can be expected to molest, harass, or coerce, or in any way fail to cooperate politically with, those one supposes will be damned. Embedded in Rawls's historical account is evidently a set of psychological and sociological *assumptions* about the relationship between religious belief and political behaviour, according to which some religious beliefs are considered congruent with liberal citizenship, others not. This set of assumptions leads Rawls to conclude that there is a conflict, perhaps absolute— note the phrase 'if not impossible' above—between a traditional and not uncommon religious belief (damnation), on the one hand, and liberal citizenship, on the other.

Of course there is a great difference between retrospectively acknowledging the happy consequences for liberalism of the disappearance of certain religious beliefs, on the one hand, and *intending* the disappearance of these beliefs by means, for example, of a programme of religious propaganda or mandatory government education, on the other. Liberalism may happily result in the attenuation of certain religious beliefs, but this does not mean that liberalism is committed to taking active measures to restrict those beliefs. It is clear that Rawls believes that the disappearance of some religious beliefs was good and even necessary for liberalism. But does he believe that liberal governments should actively 'clear the way' for liberalism by limiting the diversity of religious beliefs?

In another revealing passage, Rawls leaves no doubt as to his answer to that question: 'Political liberalism . . . supposes that a reasonable comprehensive doctrine does not reject the essentials of a democratic regime. Of course, a society may also contain *unreasonable and irrational, and even mad, comprehensive doctrines*. In their case *the problem is to contain them so* they do not undermine the unity and justice of society' [my emphasis] (xviii–xix). What are the democratic essentials which citizens must believe if they are not to be considered 'unreasonable and irrational' or worse? What does Rawls mean by 'irrational' or 'mad' comprehensive doctrines? Whatever they are, Rawls says in an ominous afterthought that they pose so serious a threat to the 'unity and justice' of society that the problem is to 'contain' them; at another point, he notes that such 'doctrines' are comparable to 'war and disease,' and that their very existence 'gives us the practical task of containing them' (64 n. 19).

In expressly applying the agitated Cold-War language of 'containment' to 'unreasonable,' 'irrational,' and 'mad' comprehensive doctrines, Rawls is again not referring to militant fundamentalisms or revolutionary religions, at least not primarily. For Rawls's 'reasonableness,' the central concept of *Political Liberalism*, is in fact a remarkably high standard. To qualify as reasonable, a comprehensive doctrine must accept much more than the principle of religious liberty, for example, or basic democratic institutions. All that is not enough: comprehensive doctrines must also accept the 'burdens of judgment.' To do so, a comprehensive doctrine must accept that reasonable people disagree about a variety of questions of judgment and fact. The result is a mild form of fallibilism: to be reasonable, a comprehensive doctrine must in effect acknowledge that there are good reasons for denying its own truth-claims, because there is much to be said on all sides.

What makes Rawls's liberalism remarkably exclusionary if not 'sectarian,' is that the burdens of judgment displace firm religious faith. According to various religious orthodoxies, of course, religious truth is mediated by revelation through faith, yielding an unshakable confidence. The main historical religions, which Rawls says he hopes can embrace his political conception of justice (170), therefore cannot accept the burdens of judgment. It follows that on Rawls's view these widely practised religions are unreasonable and would thus be unable to enter an overlapping consensus on justice as fairness and, perhaps, would even need to be 'contained'. For fundamental to Rawls's political theory is his view that the only just and stable society is the uniformly 'reasonable' society made up of uniformly 'reasonable' individuals, who are not divided or conflicted in their loyalties but rather 'wholehearted' liberal citizens. Such citizens do not merely obey the laws of liberal society but do so 'for the right reasons' (xxxix–xl)—which they can do, of course, only if they are 'reasonable.'

Whatever Rawls's intentions, the implications for religious pluralism are clear: Rawlsian liberalism requires the containment of religious within the bounds of 'reasonableness.' Of course, Rawls does not spell out how this could be carried out consistently with liberal principles. However, at a minimum, presumably the stability of the institutions embodying these principles could justify, for example, the use of mandatory government schooling to 'contain' the influence of 'unreasonable' religious opinions.[12] Perhaps containment might extend to the suppression of political parties organised around 'unreasonable' and hence 'undemocratic' doctrines—a practice not unheard of in the United States. Political liberalism would seem to support, if not require, the ongoing containment of religion to keep the world safe for liberalism.

To put the point another way: despite Rawls's vigorous efforts over many years to adapt his liberal theory to the real-world circumstance of deeply divided societies, it is striking how unsuitable it remains even for the society whose political intuitions, institutions, and history it is most meant to reflect: the United States. The structure of Rawls's liberal theory suggests an explanation: with certain narrow goals and premises locked into place at the start, particularly concerning reasonableness, political justification, the presumed illiberalism of religion, 'public reason,' and the overriding importance of political values, it is not surprising that Rawls should ultimately consider pluralism—the real pluralism that obtains in the real world—a threat to be contained.

Rawls follows the characteristically liberal path, blazed by Grotius, and paved by Hobbes, Locke, Pufendorf, and others: that of forcing the vast diversity of actual religious professions and practices into the uniform liberal mould of 'peaceableness' or 'reasonableness.' The historic liberal path remains widely followed, even though its radical inadequacy has long been noted: commenting as early as 1677 on the larger homogenising project of early modern liberalism, of which the containment of religious pluralism was but one component, Leibniz replied to Hobbes and Pufendorf—two of Grotius' greatest disciples—that no known political society exhibited the cultural and institutional uniformity they took for granted.

Beyond the Conflict between Grotian Liberalism and Religious Pluralism

The ultimate aim of Grotius' strikingly influential theological efforts was to generate an overlapping Christian consensus capable of meeting the challenge of radical religious pluralism. More specifically, the aim of the Grotian consensus was to solve what John Gray has aptly called the 'liberal problem': 'that of specifying terms of peaceful coexistence among exponents of rival, and perhaps rationally incommensurable, world-views . . .'[13] This is a *liberal* problem because liberals, in seriously contending that rival world-views *should* be allowed to co-exist both freely and peacefully, must also hold that it is somehow *possible in principle* for them to do so: *ought* implies *can*. Through his overlapping consensus, Grotius specifies the basis on which diverse religious conceptions—even non-religious ones—can co-exist peacefully and harmoniously. In his important article on Rawls, Wenar[14] supposes that '[t]he idea of an overlapping consensus is Rawls's own . . .' '[I]t seems unanticipated in the history of political theory . . .' I have in effect suggested that Wenar's historical supposition is incorrect: while Grotius did not of course have the idea of an overlapping consensus in the full-blown Rawlsian form, he did anticipate it in important ways.

More importantly, I have tried to show that while Grotius' overlapping consensus was an astonishingly creative solution to the 'liberal problem,' it could not succeed without containing—and radically constraining—religious pluralism. Why the demands of liberal politics can demand the containment of religion, Grotius states bluntly in one of his later writings: 'It is better to be a good citizen than a good Christian.' Rawls articulates a strikingly similar claim in language only slightly less blunt: political values and institutions define 'the very groundwork of our existence,' he writes, and thus 'normally have sufficient weight to override all other values that may come in conflict with them' (138–139). Liberalism can legitimately contain religious pluralism because, in the end, the values of liberalism are trumps.

Grotius' thought, remarkably like the political thought of Rawls in terms of its genesis and purpose, and remarkably influential in bringing a distinctive political tradition into being, helps explain the continuing conflictual relationship between 'Grotian' liberalism and religious pluralism. For, after all, understanding liberalism properly requires understanding it historically. And understood historically, the liberal tradition Grotius helped to found is not and has never been 'neutral', but has always fought vociferously to make the world safe for a certain kind of morality, a certain kind of personality, a certain kind of society.

The conflict between 'Grotian' liberalism and religious pluralism is, of course, acutely relevant to the politics not only of the West, but of countries across the globe. At the beginning of this essay we noted Shklar's observation that liberalism originated 'in the terrible tension within Christianity between the demands of creedal orthodoxy and those of charity, between faith and

136

morality.' According to Grotius, only when this tension was resolved decisively against traditional 'orthodoxy' and in favor of 'morality' could the business of making the world liberal safely begin. Perhaps little has changed. For a terrible tension evident in our time is a tension quite similar to the one described by Shklar. This is the tension between the demands of globally resurgent, muscular, and revivalist 'orthodoxies,' and what many people around the world take to be the demands of 'morality': liberty, peaceableness, and reasonableness. Today, in the face of the revivalist orthodoxies that constitute the world-wide *revanche de Dieu*,' it is unclear how the ongoing business of making—and keeping—the world safe for liberalism can proceed. For example, how partisans of liberalism and would-be global democratisers are best to understand and address the contemporary 'Islamic Resurgence' in particular remains far from clear. According to Samuel Huntington, the single best guide to understanding the politicised Islamic Resurgence of today is Michael Walzer's 1965 book on the politicised Calvinism of the 17th century, *The Revolution of the Saints*. If so, and *if* we are convinced of the 'reasonableness' of the business of making the world safe for liberalism, perhaps the single best guide to what may need to be done to tame 'unreasonable' Islam today is the work of the man who contributed as much as anyone to the taming of 'unreasonable' (i.e. Calvinist) Christianity then: Hugo Grotius.[15]

If we are not convinced of the reasonableness of the 'Grotian' liberal project, it may be because we have concluded that it is more humane and less utopian to resist any project that attempts a definitive resolution of this terrible tension, one way or the other. If that is our conclusion, then our search will be for a politics that preserves, not resolves, the tension between political liberalism and religious pluralism in its various forms. Such a politics would in effect be a minimal liberalism and religious pluralism in its various forms. Such a politics would in effect be a minimal liberalism that leans less towards Grotian liberalism and its discourse of philosophical authority and more towards democracy and its presumptive respect for all non-violent forms of political participation and all political participants who respect the minimum conditions of democracy. Alfred Stepan aptly describes these conditions as the 'twin tolerations,' according to which, in effect, the state must respect the autonomy of religious institutions (including their freedom to express themselves politically) and religious institutions must respect the autonomy of the state. An otherwise open democratic politics—open to the irreducible plurality of human goods, open to the irreducible plurality of religious and cultural communities, open to the diverse constitutional means of respecting these goods and these communities—will avoid the pitfalls of a self-defeating strategy of liberal containment, which is as likely to provoke the radicalisation of religion (as well as contempt for liberalism) as its pacification, and which, in an age of 'identity politics,' can in any case keep the lid on religious pluralism for only so long. Lloyd and Susanne Rudolphs' vivid account of India's 'cultural federalism,' in this book, whereby Indian law balances universalism with a pluralism that attaches legal identity to distinct religio-cultural communities, and James Tully's work on 'constitutional dialogues' among distinct cultural communities in North America, show in their different ways what such a politics might look like. Particularly in religiously diverse societies, a politics that in these and other ways makes as much room as possible for democratic bargaining as against the limited discourse of liberal arguing is in fact more likely to capture the properly liberal spirit: generosity.

Acknowledgment

I have incurred many debts in writing this chapter, especially to Alfred Stepan, James Piscatori, David Marquand; and the September 1999 conference participants, whose penetrating questions and comments demanded better answers than I could give at the time or can give now. Most of all, I wish to thank Rebecca Samuel Shah.

Notes

1 Judith Shklar, 'The Liberalism of Fear,' in Nancy Rosenblum, ed., *Liberalism and the Moral Life*, Cambridge, Massachusetts, Harvard University Press, 1989, p. 23.

2 Hugo Grotius, *Meletius sive de iis quae inter Christianos conveniunt epistola*, G. H. M. Posthumus Meyjes, trans. Leiden, E. J. Brill, 1988. I cite the *Meletius* by paragraph number; my own translations sometimes depart from those of Meyjes.

3 Hugo Grotius, *De iure belli ac pacis libri tres* (*On the Law of War and Peace, Three Books*), Francis Kelsey, trans. Oxford, Clarendon Press, 1925, Prolegomena, ¶11.

4 For this point and the reference to Grotius' letter to Walaeus, I am indebted to Richard Tuck, *Philosophy and Government: 1572–1651* Cambridge, Cambridge University Press, 1993), pp. 186–187.

5 Hugo Grotius, *Opera omnia theologica* (London, 1679), vol. III, p. 679, quoted and translated in Tuck, *Philosophy and Government*, pp. 200–201.

6 Hugo Grotius, *Opera Omnia Theologica* London, 1679, vol. IV, p. 701, quoted and translated in G. H. M. Posthumus Meyjes, 'Hugo Grotius as an irenicist,' in Robert Feenstra, ed., *The World of Hugo Grotius* (1583–1645) Amsterdam, APA-Holland University Press, 1984, p. 63.

7 The idea of religious 'multi-vocality' I borrow from Alfred Stepan, 'The World's Religious Systems and Democracy: Crafting the "Twin Tolerations," forthcoming in his *Arguing Comparative Politics* Oxford & New York, Oxford University Press, 2000, pp. 20–21. On the multi-vocality of 16th and 17th century Calvinism, see the important work of David Little: *Religion, Order, and Law*. 2nd ed. Chicago: The University of Chicago Press, 1984 and 'Reformed Faith and Religious Liberty,' in Donald McKim, ed., *Major Themes in the Reformed Tradition* Grand Rapids, Michigan: Eerdmans, 1992, pp. 196–213.

8 Grotius concludes the *Meletius* by approvingly quoting the theologian Salvianus to this effect, at ¶91. In Locke, see, for example, the James Tully ed., *A Letter Concerning Toleration*, Indianapolis, Hacket Publishing Company, 1983, p. 38 and passim.

9 John Rawls, *Political Liberalism*, paperback ed. New York: Columbia University

Press, 1996, pp. xxxix–xl. Subsequent page references in the text are to *Political Liberalism*.

10 John Rawls, *The Law of Peoples* Cambridge, Massachusetts, Harvard University Press, 1999, pp. 19–22.

11 Samuel Huntington, *The Clash of Civilizations and the Remaking of World Order* New York, Simon & Schuster, 1996, p. 217.

12 In fact, the containment of religious diversity has historically been a function of American government ('public') schools, which were founded partly for the purpose of containing the Catholicism of millions of 19th-century Irish, German, and (later) Southern European immigrants: many Americans of the time feared that Catholicism would otherwise subvert liberal democracy. Because of such fears, Protestant-controlled state legislatures not only prohibited state funding of 'sectarian' (i.e. Catholic) schools, but also mandated that government schools promote the 'common (i.e. Protestant) religion.' 'Common School' movements arose in France and Holland at about the same time, and were intended to serve a similar 'containment' function. For a fascinating comparative study, see Charles Glenn, *The Myth of the Common School*, Amherst, Massachusetts, The University of Massachusetts Press, 1987.

13 John Gray, *Liberalism*, Minneapolis, University of Minnesota Press, 1995, p. 85.

14 Leif Wenar, '*Political Liberalism*: An Internal Critique,' *Ethics*, October 1995, pp. 33–4.

15 Ronald Nettler's fascinating work on Mohamed Talbi expounded in his chapter in this book suggests that this contemporary Islamic theologian can perhaps be understood as the Islamic equivalent of a 'Grotian' liberal reformer.

Index

Abu-Zayd, N. H. 70
activism 79, 88, 104
Afghanistan 76, 77
Agudath Israel 40, 41
Al-Afghani, Jamal-Eddin 15
al-Azhar 70
al-Bishri, T. 61
al-Bustani, Boutrus 15
al-Ghannouchi, Rachid 17
al-Ghazzali, M. 69
al-Haqq, J. 70
Anabaptists 10
Ankerberg, J. 86
anti-clericalism 64, 112
anti-communism 98–9
Arendt, H. 12
Arminius, J. 123
Asiatic Society of Bengal 22
Ataturk, K. 71–2
Audard, C. 14
Augustine, St 5
Aum Shinrikyo 104
Austin, G. 30, 32
Ayubi, N. 62

Bahadur Shah II 26
Bakker, J. 80, 82, 85–6
Bakker, T. 80, 86
Balaji v State of Mysore [1963] 20–1
Bank of Scotland 85
Bano, S. 34
Barber, B. 2
Bayle, P. 113
Beatles 87
Beck, T. 27
Ben-Gurion, D. 43–4
Bentinck, W. 24
Bernhardt, R. 17
Bharatiya Janta Party (BJP) 32, 35
Bismarck, O. von 111
Blachere, R. 51
Bonhöffer, D. 14
Bourdieu, P. 96
Bradlaugh, C. 7

Brown, P. 5
Bruni, L. 11
Bulaç, A. 17
Bush, G. 82, 84
Bush, G. Jr 81

Calvinism 123–5, 129–30, 131–2
  and liberalism 130
Campiche, R. J. 96
Carter, J. 82
Castro, F. 101
Catholic Church 90, 91, 96, 97, 111
Chamberlain, H. S. 118
charisma 60–2
Christian democratic parties 90, 93, 97–8,
  101–2
Christian fundamentalism 79–88
Christian Right 80–8, 108
  as big business 85–6
  as minority 82
  followers 82, 87
  political power 82–4
church and state 1, 5, 11–12, 91–2, 104–19
church authority 96–7
churches
  and identity 94
  as rallying points 93
  rites de passage 92
Church of England 91, 101, 107
Clinton, W. 2, 82
Cole, G. D. H. 112
Colebrook, H. T. 23
Combes, E. 111
communal reservations 28–9
community 94–5
concessionism 110–13
conformity 96–7
Coupland, R. 27
Cruise, T. 87
cultural federalism 3, 21–3

Dalhousie, R. J. 24
Daniel, N. 15
Davie, G. 92, 93

Religion and Democracy

15